the LIGHT ABOVE

Sarah Margaret Fuller (1810–1850)

the LIGHT ABOVE

A MEMOIR WITH MARGARET FULLER

MARIA DINTINO

SHANTI ARTS PUBLISHING
BRUNSWICK, MAINE

THE LIGHT ABOVE
A Memoir with Margaret Fuller

Published by Shanti Arts Publishing

Book interior designed by Shanti Arts Designs

Cover image by Keegan Monahan, *Morning Star*

Cover front designed by Jenna Cea-Curry

Shanti Arts LLC
193 Hillside Road
Brunswick, Maine 04011
www.shantiarts.com

Printed in the United States of America

This is a work of creative nonfiction. As the Preface makes clear, Maria's chapters are about the author as she remembers her life; Margaret's chapters are the author's interpretation of Margaret Fuller and her life. The author has tried to recreate events, locales, and conversations from her memories of them. In order to maintain anonymity, the names of some individuals and places have been changed. Conversations are not intended to be word-for-word transcripts but rather are written to evoke appropriate feeling and meaning.

ISBN: 978-1-956056-22-8 (softcover)
ISBN: 978-1-956056-23-5 (digital)

Library of Congress Control Number: 2021952165

To my entire large and loving family,
especially my beautiful parents
who always leave love's light on.

If you have knowledge, let others light their candles in it.

—Margaret Fuller (1810–1850)

CONTENTS

PREFACE

I WAS AT A LOSS. I HAD UNBURIED THIS PERSON AND DIDN'T know what to do with her.

What was I going to do with all of the information and my infatuation with this woman, Margaret Fuller, who was born over two hundred years ago? I had read everything written by her—her books, columns, and letters—and almost everything written about her—scholarly biographies, essays, and more.

Early one morning while awake in bed, it came to me quite unexpectedly that I was to write from the heart. Something told me I was trying too hard to figure out a how, a what. Instead, I was to go inside and allow what was percolating to work itself from there.

Sitting myself down and writing Margaret from the heart became a story about me too. Why me? Leave me out of this, I thought. But no, it was not to be. I was not allowed to write her story without writing my own because I had unburied two women.

One would think telling your own story would be straightforward. I was there. It was me. But it's not easy, and I was called back day after day to move in closer.

Maria's chapters are about me as I remember my life. Margaret's are my interpretation of her and her life. They are not her words; they are not her thoughts. They are my interpretation of her words and thoughts, my interpretation of who she was and is, my interpretation of her feelings and experiences based on what I learned of her. I ingested what I could and wrote from that well of information. I tried to stay true to my connection with her, to portray my awe and respect and not misrepresent her.

I wrote Margaret from the inside out, and through this process, I discovered the life guide I had always longed for. And for that, I am a better, stronger person and am eternally grateful.

You knowing who Margaret Fuller is after reading this is success. You telling others about this remarkable woman surpasses my mission. And you discovering anything about yourself through reading this memoir hits it right out of the park.

INTRODUCTION

Big, dark ribs resting on bleached white sand. A massive chunk of ship loosened by upheaval and delivered by the tide.

Locals informed us when we relocated to St. Augustine, Florida, in 2015 that there hadn't been a direct hit from a hurricane in over twenty years. Days after our first year, Hurricane Matthew hit. It was terrifying and heartbreakingly damaging. The following year, 2017, Irma hit. In March of 2018, the remnants of a ship, aptly named the Spring Break Wreck, appeared. It is assumed the storms freed it up after being buried for years and slowly hoisted it to shore.

I couldn't help but wonder whether this could be part of the *Elizabeth*, the ship Margaret Fuller went down in off the shores of Fire Island in 1850. Though from the 1800s, the Spring Break Wreck was constructed of wood found here in the southeastern United States, so probably not. Apparently, once the ocean swallows something and it's not rescued, retrieved, or washed ashore, it remains in the ocean, often for a very long time. Even forever.

Still new here, walking the beach and thinking in the expansive way the ocean challenges one to think, I developed an attraction to the conch shell. I only had eyes for the conch, the sacred *Shankha*. Periodically, an intact conch shell would appear, as I'm sure they do for others, but these started to appear when I needed them.

One afternoon, while reeling from the news that my sister's husband had left her after almost thirty years of marriage, I walked along the beach, shrouded in shock and sadness. It was a busy day at this beach, and I was weaving in and out of people, especially little children who often neglect to look up as they run from the playful waters. A conch shell washed up at my feet. I looked down at it, then looked around to see if others saw it. No one noticed, so I picked it up, guiltily claiming it. I knew it was for Laura, and I thanked the ocean. Holding it snug in my hand, I walked along, tears streaming.

A couple weeks later, my daughter called to tell me her good friend's mother had died suddenly. Her friend, McKenzie, and her mother were very close, and it was a devastating blow to the entire family. My daughter was clearly shaken by it and so was I. Saddened, I again found myself walking the beach, thinking of McKenzie. It wasn't crowded on the beach that day. Being later in the afternoon, I imagined many beachgoers had already departed. Several women were scouring the shores with bags to carry the shells they'd find, so I didn't expect to find much, but I had developed a love for the conch and was always on the prowl.

Almost back to where I had started, I spotted something ahead, glinting in the sun. I approached to discover a large conch shell in pristine condition. I looked around in amazement. How could this be? How did these other women hunting on the beach miss this perfect specimen in plain sight? I picked it up, puzzled. I recognized that it was for McKenzie and thanked the ocean.

It was then that she made it known that it was her, Margaret Fuller, offering the shells and not the ocean itself. I was struck by this truth. Think what you may, but when you know, you know.

Before we moved here, before I walked the beaches and ships and shells washed up on the shores, there was an encounter. It was a crisp, starry night in New Hampshire, a day or two before Christmas, one of those days leading up to the holiday that sparkles. My sister, Theresa, and her family were in town. The fact that they lived in California and were not able to visit often added to the magical quality of that day.

Theresa had recently been merged as a diviner—a stick diviner in the Dagara tradition. This was a huge deal both for her and all of us. Not only were we proud and in awe of her, but Theresa—always possessing gifts of listening, knowing, and compassion from the youngest age—being a diviner felt so right.

As Dad prepared the evening meal, Theresa and my daughter, Annie, and I headed upstairs for my first divination. I had no idea what to expect, but I was eager for the experience and grateful for Theresa's offer, knowing how precious her time was while visiting.

In the gambrel of golden light that was our childhood home, we huddled in the smallest bedroom, the one my brothers shared years back. We sat on pillows, crowding what little floor space there was, our knees almost touching. With Annie taking notes, me holding one end of the stick and my sister the other, we began. I followed Theresa's lead as she relayed to me messages and requests from ancestors and others. Before long, a woman appeared. My sister didn't know who it was and asked me who I thought it could be. The woman was asking for something, for me to do something. From the looks of the woman, her hair and dress, Theresa wondered if it was Emily Dickinson. We questioned whether it might be one of the Brontë sisters. Then I knew. I was sure it was Margaret Fuller.

I had been introduced to Margaret in graduate school in a course on Transcendentalism and the literary figures of Concord, Massachusetts, in the 1800s. At the time, we read Margaret's book *Woman in the Nineteenth Century*, but for me, it was overshadowed by the works of Ralph Waldo Emerson and especially by Henry David Thoreau, so much so that by the end of the semester, I had labeled myself a Thoreauvian.

Following the divination, I was surprised to discover Margaret's book still on my bookshelf. I was amused to see that I had marked it heavily, both with highlighters and pens, and had written comments in the margins. Funny that I hadn't absorbed more of its significance then. Why had I tucked it away while keeping Thoreau's *Walden* always at hand, for sanity and inspiration?

Yes, it seemed there was something to be done. That December night, Margaret relayed to my sister, who in turn relayed to me, an urgency of sorts. That was six years ago.

It has been a circuitous journey, the unfurling and reconnecting, the expansion and contraction, the beating of a heart, the spiral of a shell.

ONE

Maria

I'M SURE MY FATHER MET THE CALL FROM THE HOSPITAL with a heavy dose of happiness, along with a measure of disappointment. After all, I was the third daughter in a row on the way to the desired son. I often teased my younger sister, the fourth announcement of a daughter, that she was met with even more disappointment, but somehow that became untrue because she ultimately became the youngest daughter and an adorable blond in a sea of brunettes.

Me, I was number three. I've always loved that number, but in the familial line-up, it didn't mean much. I'm not saying my parents didn't love me because I've always known they did. Those two have enough love to circle the world many times. But time and attention are limited, no matter what. And with six children in seven years and all the other responsibilities of parenting and running a household, there was not enough to go around. The quieter child with no special place in the sibling line-up was unlikely to get what she needed or what any child needs—some sort of notice from an adult in her world.

My dad named his first child after his favorite teacher, Sister Cecilia. We had the privilege of meeting Sister Cecilia a few years back, and she had the surprise of learning all those years later that one of her pupils named his daughter after her. Even with Sister Cecilia being an old woman, it was easy to see why Dad made that decision. As the oldest child, Cecilia did not disappoint. She was a feisty little thing who, according to Mom, was potty trained and walking well before she was one.

This was good because along came Laura, number two daughter, who proved to be the opposite of her older sister, not walking until she was almost two. Quite early on, Laura became Dad's first boy, with her confident and no-nonsense approach to life. She mowed the lawn, helped in the garden, and went on plowing gigs in the winter. With that John Denver denim hat atop long, dark ponytails, she was someone you could count on to get the job done.

Then I came along. I hear I was a beautiful baby, and although there's only one photograph of me (one more than of my younger sister), it does support that claim. I was chosen as the model baby in the hospital, the one used to demonstrate to all the new mothers how to change a diaper and swaddle a newborn.

In October of the following year, Theresa was born and I was no longer the youngest—Theresa claimed that position in the family. She was like a Kewpie doll, a wisp of blond hair and plump little cheeks that especially stood out when she smiled. She'd walk up and down the street pushing her doll stroller, greeting each of us with her trademark "Bout hi." When Theresa was in first grade, we'd arrive at school and her classmates would run up to her, begging to hold her hands and walk her into the schoolyard like she was royalty. There was something there.

Then came Carmine, named after Dad's beloved brother who didn't make it home from WWII, perishing on the beaches of Normandy on D-Day. What a thrill to have a son in this large Italian family and to name him after the greatest loss this family had ever sustained. How this must have brought such joy and love into the hearts of all our family. I can only imagine the celebration in the neighborhood, the cigars and drinks, and the relief to my mom, who had finally delivered a blue bundle. And an industrious little guy he was, always full of energy—so much so that he used to run in place so fast he became a blur. We called this his "twitcho act."

Then the youngest, a little brother for Carmine. The story is that I named David. Somehow, I shouted out that name as we all crowded around Mom, who was soliciting suggestions. David was our plaything, we girls poking and prodding at him from the day he arrived home. Our "jolly ollie" David entertained us from the start.

The love was there, the love from above and between. But the time factor can only yield so much, and staying on top of the day-to-day logistics forced some of the secondary needs to the side.

It wasn't until I was in kindergarten that it was discovered I could not hear well. I recall that day, sitting in the classroom with my back to the teacher, Mrs. Armstrong. I had a barrette in my hair that I was crazy about. It was plastic with a tortoiseshell pattern and a gold cursive "Maria" imprinted on it. Oh, that barrette! All mine because no one else was going to wear a barrette with my name on it. When someone asked my name, I proudly pointed to it.

That day, Mrs. Armstrong realized I could not hear because when my back was to her and she called my name, I did not respond. She informed my parents. My mother had some suspicions, but with all that was going on, she hadn't had a chance to investigate. Fortunately, my hard-of-hearing situation was cleared up quite readily with minor surgery and dreaded weekly runs to the ear doctor to get my ears "blown out." With a lisp and some difficulty with pronunciation, I was re-released to the world.

This world we inhabited while growing up was insular. We spent all our time with each other and rarely had friends over or spent time at friends' houses, primarily because our mother didn't drive and our father worked two jobs. We became each other's soulmates and irritants, but all in all, it was, in its way, glorious.

Margaret

From the day I came into the world, my parents' eyes were on me in a way they would never be on my younger siblings—the ones who came next and next and so on. Losing the closest sibling in line, Julia Adelaide, so early on compounded the focus on me and sealed the deal on the burden I would carry for most of my life.

On that dark, dark day when I was but three years old, I was escorted into the room to see my little sister, Julia Adelaide, laid out perfectly on the bed, dressed as though for Sunday service with a most peaceful look on her sweet face. The adults all around me in black . . . the shadows on their faces terrifying, me knowing they knew something I didn't . . . something so horrible it made me scream and cry. I'm told I was inconsolable for the entire service and while at the cemetery where I begged them not to put Julia Adelaide in the ground, but they did it anyway, and I was scared, confused, and all alone.

What came next was up to my father. My mother was too stricken with grief to care.

First came the decision my father made that I was fit for the challenge of learning all he had learned and more. He determined that I was not only capable but gifted to withstand a rigorous homeschooling, one normally bestowed on a son. This he would never demand of any of his other children. My lessons were many and challenging, one on top of the next.

My father was correct. I was up to the challenge and could keep up with his demanding instruction. He put pressure on me, and soon I put more on myself. Most of my young life became that of the mind, often leaving my heart to long for something I could not yet describe.

This lifestyle robbed me of a common childhood, of days and hours of imaginative and freestyle play. For that, there was no time. When I needed a respite, I wandered in my mother's colorful and tenderly cared-for flower garden in the backyard. It was her annual work of beauty, and I relished in it tremendously.

Often my studies and the pressure of proving to my father that I was capable and keeping up made it difficult for me to relax or sleep. I experienced atrocious nightmares and was often found roaming the house deep in the night. I believed this unnatural experience generated the debilitating headaches that intensified as I grew older, although it could have been the curvature of my spine or my nearsightedness that were the culprits.

But I was determined that none of this would hold me back.

Maria

When my parents brought me home from the hospital as a newborn, two older sisters greeted me. They were three and two. A year and a half later, my little sister made her debut and on her heels, two little brothers. Each additional housemate required definitive space—the space that was my parents' attention and the limited physical space in a small house. My sleeping space became the stairway landing, the platform halfway up and halfway down.

Forever, middle children need to scratch their way to the air, to escape the shadows and suffocation, and to break free. My surfacing would take time and emotional acrobatics. Ah, the drama of it all.

Perhaps in a former life, I was an only child and wanted to get back there. I would, as often as possible, find a way to be by myself in a household buzzing with constant group activities and a perpetual summer-camp feel. When we played Partridge Family, my oldest sister was Shirley Jones (the mother), directing the whole production, and I would beg to be Reuben Kincaid, the band's manager with a bit part, so I could be alone on the front porch for as long as possible.

There were times when my mother tuned in to my need for space and allowed me to play in her bedroom. My parents' bedroom was off-limits. My mother ran the household with firm boundaries, with six of her own children on the loose as well as at least six more she babysat. When my eyes pleaded for a break, she granted me special permission to be in her room.

How vividly I recall sitting smack dab in the middle of her nicely made bed, brushing the hair of Laura's doll Ratty and leisurely making up a story about Ratty without anyone else chiming in or hijacking the storyline. I'm not sure how long I was alone in my parents' bedroom, but long enough to think that if I were an only child or had but one sibling, I would have my own room and could do this on a regular basis. I wouldn't have to sleep on the stairwell with little privacy, though I perhaps had more than my three sisters who all shared a room.

My mother was a labeler, especially when it came to her children. Each of us had at least one label that neatly summed us up and put us in our place. The labels may have held a grain of truth, but it's what the label omitted, what the label insinuated, that was harmful. Mine was "the pretty one." Others were "the director," "the smart one," "the rebel," "the doer," and "the baby." So, if I wasn't the smart one, did that mean I wasn't smart? If I wasn't the doer, did that mean I was a slacker?

I guess there are worse things than being the pretty one, but there had to be more to me, right? Yeah, there was a little bit more tagged on my label and it was, "She never gives us any trouble. You wouldn't even know she's there."

Most of my siblings emerged with strong identities. My oldest sister did, of course, as the oldest usually do, and for that they often pay a hefty price. My younger sister did too. She was pretty much her own person from early high school on. I remember when she would stay home on a weekend night, sewing. I would taunt her and call her a simpleton. I was flitting around, putting on makeup and trying on outfits, trying to both fit in and stand out—a boggling task. Theresa wouldn't look up and didn't respond to my name-calling. I'm sure she probably had a name or two to call me but she never did.

It wasn't that Theresa never went out and that she didn't have friends. She just didn't need to go out. It would take me many more years before I could feel good about staying in on a Friday or Saturday night.

As a child, I didn't raise my voice, didn't show signs of exceptionality, didn't misbehave, and didn't give my parents any reason to worry. I had food to eat, clean clothes to wear, and lively traditions to partake in. It was solidly good and safe. But it lacked edges. It lacked challenge and adventure.

As I embarked into life beyond what we called our "Ranch," I felt shadowy, without a grip. It wasn't long before I realized I had a hell of a lot of work to do.

Oh, there are worse things. There are such worse things that when I think of them, I want to drop to the ground and sob. But in our own lives, our things are our things, and they loom large and often consume our focus.

Margaret

I OFTEN FELT LIKE AN ONLY CHILD, ALTHOUGH I HAD MANY younger siblings. If my younger sister, Julia Adelaide, had survived, it would have been an entirely different situation, but that wasn't how life played out for me. Once she was gone, I was on my own, absorbed in the unique experience I would have as a child, the relentless pressure from Father along with the pressure I put on myself. I often thought that I did not have a childhood in the way most think of childhood. Instead, I had lessons and recitations, day and night, and I had domestic duties to help Mother with, and these included helping to care for my younger siblings.

As my childhood unfolded and the years began to pass, I found sanctuary in my learning and in books. I grew to need and want them and to see that all of this reading, thinking, writing, and reciting was becoming who I was. It was not toil as much anymore, and it was no longer lonely. In the beginning, as a young child, this lifestyle felt heavy, like chains around my ankles. I was a prisoner of my father's desires for me. But soon I discovered that this learning liberated me and propelled me into a world large enough to keep my fire burning.

This empowered me, enabling me to keep pace with the best of them, even grown men. As a child, I could hold my own in conversations and debates. I knew as much, if not more than most I met, even those students and graduates in my neighborhood from Harvard. I knew I possessed a gift—a gift for learning, for being able to eloquently share what I knew and thought, for being able to tell a story, and for readily captivating a room of people. I also knew that others, especially girls, were capable of learning much more than they were being taught or allowed to learn. I knew that knowledge would set them free, that learning leads to an understanding of oneself, and that this leads to demanding and creating a better, loftier life.

Our childhoods offer us paths—sometimes many, sometimes

few—to the rest of our lives. We can always look back and wish it were otherwise, but for what purpose? Some emerge feeling charged, ready to take on the mission of their lives; others feel unfinished or bewildered, continuing the task of discovery for years. Whatever the position, however far along one is, there's always work to be done. I was never afraid of the work, both the tasks outside of myself and the work of my head and heart. There was great pain and disappointment along with success and pure joy, but how dawns the morning without night?

I knew from early on that the whole point of life was to grow and that was my constant aim.

Maria

Rare was the day I didn't go for a walk. Walking time was sacred time, especially when I was alone. Sometimes my walks included a destination—to work or the store. Most often and most lovely were those devoid of destination except where I found myself in my mind.

When I was growing up, our dirt driveway was often empty, no car sitting on its dusty surface. With our father working two jobs and having more of a social life than any of us had outside the home, the car was more often than not in various parking lots in our little city than in its home spot. Our driveway became a bicycle parking lot, full of our bikes and those belonging to the neighborhood kids. There came a point in the late afternoon when Mom would holler for us to move our bikes because when Dad did come home, he wouldn't be happy to find the driveway impassable.

But even more telling than the driveway being packed with parked bicycles was the amount of walking we did. We had to. Mom didn't drive, and even if she had, the one vehicle we owned was often unavailable. So we "hoofed it." In the early years, it was not uncommon to see my mother with a baby carriage and four young girls hanging on to the sides as it moved down the sidewalk. Or my mother in the rear holding David's hand (the youngest) while we buddied up and walked along in front of her, heading to the store or to visit a relative a few blocks away.

As we got older, we were allowed to walk places in twos and threes, especially to school and the playground in the summer. I remember just about every crack in the sidewalk on the way to elementary school about a mile from our home; the Island and Winchester Street bridges in all seasons, sometimes the river shockingly shallow and smelly, other times forcefully flowing with ice crisps on the edges. I remember the hilly dirt path through Hickey-Desilets Park that spared us a long, drawn-out corner, and crossing the railroad tracks when trains still ran through Keene. Our neighbor, an engineer, would throw us candy and honk the loud, deep whistle for our amusement. And finally, I remember turning onto Wilson Street, lined with shrubs and houses that seemed sacred just because they were closer to the church, then crossing onto the school grounds, friends and teachers there to welcome us.

My mother, back home, didn't worry much because she just didn't worry much, and walking was what most children did before families had more than one car and most schools were still neighborhood schools.

Margaret

My happiest memories are of me prancing around my mother's flower gardens in our backyard in Cambridge. I would do a skip-walk, hair bouncing, feet tapping, never taking my eyes off the beauty of the brightly colored flowers and the bees buzzing them. Round and round I'd go, enthralled and feeling more and more released and giddy as I circled, now and then stopping to closely examine a blossom from every angle possible.

Being in a city forces one to walk, perhaps more than the rural areas, at least to get to one place or another. As I grew and made connections in town, I would walk with Mother and some of my siblings here and there and even by myself on occasion.

In my teens, I was allowed to walk to familiar places where people were expecting me. But always these walks were about more than getting from one place to another, more than being released at one end and welcomed at the other. These walks became time to commune with nature and with the world outside of my house—other houses, buildings, and shops. These walks were sanctuaries not bound by restrictions, propriety, and stifling air. The ceiling was the sky, the floor a carpet of grass or trodden dirt, the walls a smattering of waving trees and bushes that housed the thrilling music of birds. These places between, from doorstep to doorstep, although not the beauty and perfection I longed for, lightened my sometimes melancholy mood.

These same routes at night could take my breath away. The

sparkling night sky and moonlight changed everything, blanketing the town in a serenity hard to find during the bright light of day.

I came to need and cherish moonlight.

Maria

KAREN LOVED TO BE AT OUR HOUSE, AND I CHERISHED THE moments I spent at Karen's house. For most of her childhood, Karen was an only child, and that was unusual then . . . and as far as I was concerned, desirable. I could not imagine having my own room and being the only one my parents focused on, the only one to talk about my day at the dinner table, and the only one they had to buy things for.

Both of Karen's parents worked, so my mother, who didn't work outside of the home, would babysit her and many others. To Karen, it was paradise, especially since she fit right in with our line-up, right between me and my older sister Laura. And she had the imagination to keep up with all of us, especially my oldest sister, Cecilia, the director of all our productions.

Playing Partridge Family was one of our go-to backyard and porch activities, and Karen got to be Susan Dey or Laurie, which I envied. I got to be Delilah, Danny's twin sister, or Reuben, the manager, which I preferred so I could be alone for much of the game. But Karen was right in there with Shirley Jones, Cecilia, David Cassidy, Laura, and they were the ones who planned out the entire episode while the rest of us goofed around, waiting to hear what our scenes and lines would be.

When we weren't playing Partridge Family, we'd be engaged in other imaginative play that involved singing, dancing, and acting. Other times, kickball and hide-and-seek would steal the show. It was always a highlight when I was asked to go to Karen's house with her when she needed to grab something. It was just around the corner from our house so my mother usually agreed that one or more of us could accompany Karen for a few minutes. She had her own key, whereas we never locked our door; and she had a purple, banana-seat, stingray bicycle, and we had old-fashioned, English-style Rollfasts. Envy filled my being.

The house was usually dark, the blinds closed tight. Yes, Karen had air conditioning, while we argued over the positioning of one box fan in the hallway at our house. We'd walk through the darkened living room and down the small hallway, first to the kitchen, where Karen could actually go into the refrigerator! We weren't allowed to open the refrigerator, at least not without permission. And Karen would hand us individually wrapped cheese slices, a wonder beyond wonder. It was not only a treat to eat a slice of cheese that wasn't in a sandwich, but to unwrap a slice slowly and savor it . . . splendid!

From there, we'd go to her room to grab whatever it was she needed. Her room. All decked out in purples and pinks; her collection of horse figurines lined up on the white headboard. I was never that into horses, but I admired that collection. Karen would lift each horse and tell me its name. Some had reins and saddles, others were bareback and wild. If I had those horses or any kind of collection like it, I'd want to stay right there and play, but Karen would rather be in the mix of all of us putting on shows and racing around the yard like a pack of hyenas.

When Karen's mom would arrive in her nurse's uniform late in the afternoon to pick her up, Karen didn't want to leave, and we didn't want her to. We'd get on our knees in the kitchen and beg her to let Karen stay until dinnertime. Usually, Karen's mother would acquiesce unless they had somewhere else to be. Karen was like our sister, but secretly I wished I were Karen—sister-less.

Years later, Karen's mom had two more little girls, and Karen was no longer an only. I don't remember ever asking Karen how she felt about that, but I guess I figured she was fine with it, probably even happy about it. She always seemed to prefer to be around others, not by herself, and I suppose it shifted the focus off of her, which may have been a relief. Sometimes it's too much pressure, too much breathing down the neck, just too much for one kid to handle.

Margaret

My younger siblings—five brothers and a sister—had an entirely different experience than I did. When I was twenty-three, my father moved us to a farm in Groton, Massachusetts, and along with their schooling and my tutoring them, these brothers of mine had to get up early in the dark, cold New England mornings to tend to the cows and do other chores. My father, who had traded politics and law for a good dose of farm living, expected them to be his farmhands and believed this lifestyle would make them not only smart (for we were determined they would attend Harvard, just like their father) but strong and steadfast.

Now and then they would rebel. They did not want to do this kind of work every day, they did not want to get up before sunrise and deal with such drudgery. As they grew, they stopped helping Father as much as he needed them. But what could I say? I had rebelled too. I did not like living on the farm. I had rejected our father's decision as well.

When we first moved from Boston to this rural town, to this farm, I was angry. I did not want to leave my circle behind, all my connections and access to the bustling that the cities of Boston and Cambridge offered. How could Father do this to us? I was the one who outwardly let him know how unhappy I was with the decision. It seemed selfish to me that because he was at a point in his career where he desired a change, he had to drag his entire family to a place that offered less opportunity and society. How did he feel this would benefit us?

To make some sort of amends, Father constructed a seat for me on a prime spot of land that he labeled Margaret's Grove. He envisioned I would retreat there to think and read, and in some way that would alleviate the anger I harbored for being ripped from my social and intellectual circles. I hardly acknowledged this structure built solely for me, which, considering there were so many of us, was a thoughtful gesture. I never gave him the satisfaction of seeing me sit there reading.

I always had a desire to be more and to do more. The move to this farm installed yet another barrier to my desires, another obstacle in addition to my being a female and not possessing adequate resources. Yet with a revelation I experienced after Thanksgiving service when my frustration boiled over and sent me running from the church in a confused rage, I realized that fighting my lot in this way was not going to serve me well. Instead, doing what I could in genuine service to my family and others would enable me to come home to myself and focus on projects I could accomplish. This restored my faith that, one way or another, this would work itself out. Forward movement is often imperceptible when it's ever so slow, but in my mind and heart, I proclaimed my acceptance of the universe and trusted in its care.

By dedicating myself more to tutoring my siblings and helping with chores around the home, I became part of the entire mechanism that made things work. I regained my balance and a sense of peace and hope.

Then I became sick, and for a few days, it looked bleak. Father sat on my bed and told me in no uncertain terms that he was proud of me—something he had never said before—and that he knew I was good. Not perfect but truly good. When I recovered, I kept his words close. Then he became ill and within days, he passed. I was devastated.

Occasionally, I sat with a book in the sanctuary my father had built for me, but I didn't open it. I held it to my chest and let the tears run down my cheeks. I thanked Father, for although being his subject was difficult, the bottom line was he saw potential in me and believed in me. I imagined him being in charge was sometimes a lonely and intimidating position as well. I believed he did what he felt was best for his family, providing us with fresher air and a heartier existence on the farm. I wished he had lived long enough to see his sons graduate Harvard; his daughter, Ellen, marry. And me—oh, how I wish he could have seen me accomplish all that I did.

Maria

My greatest fear growing up was that my father would die, that he would have a heart attack or trip down the stairs. We needed him and he seemed the most vulnerable.

Dad was a huge presence in the home, even though he wasn't there nearly as much as Mom. That we had food, lights, heat, clothes, and shoes, and whether we made it to doctor and dentist appointments, all hinged on Dad, his job, his pay, his diligence.

But none of that was on my mind when I worried Dad would die. I could not stand the thought of living without him. I needed his big love.

My grandfather, an immigrant from Italy, saved up money for my dad to go to college. Granted, college wasn't as expensive back then, but my grandfather was a janitor and had a family to support. He saved up the money for his only surviving son to attend college.

Instead of college, Dad used the money for a down payment on a house, married, and had six children. He worked a full-time job and other part-time jobs on the side to make ends meet. Although he never said he regretted his decision, his insistence that we all go to college told me he wished he had.

Mom ran a tight ship, making sure we made our beds and did our homework, disciplining us when we misbehaved or fought with each other, and assigning chores so we each pulled our weight around the house. I am in awe of how she managed the day-to-day goings-on of our busy, crowded household. But Dad brought the tenderness. He was the romantic. This was especially evident in his love for musicals. He made us listen to them over and over and watch them whenever they were televised. We didn't mind. We liked them too.

He especially liked *Camelot*, the tragedy of an ideal place, a utopia, that couldn't last. We still chuckle about the times we'd find Dad sitting in the chair late at night, after too many drinks, eyes closed, big clunky headphones on, belting out, "Camelot! Camelot!" with exaggerated fervor. We'd tiptoe by, trying not to disturb him, mostly because he'd want us to sing with him. Then we'd feel obligated to stay, his grasp on our wrist a little too strong to break away kindly.

There was hardly a Thanksgiving growing up when we didn't gather in the living room to watch *Oklahoma*, enthusiastically singing along, bellies full from the feast that included both American and Italian fare. "Oh, what a beautiful morning, oh, what a beautiful day!"

Margaret

All eyes were on me after my father passed. At twenty-five, my siblings, who had always looked to me for guidance, cast their eyes upon me with even more gravity. My mother had long since relinquished her critical role in the household, her participation quelled by the loss of two young children and a domineering husband. My mother looked to me as well.

Compounding this, because we were women, our meager resources fell into the hands of my father's brother, who found pleasure in making us wheedle for what we needed. Uncle Abraham demanded we justify all requests and then played judge, holding us in a state of worry, wondering if we had convinced him that our request was worthy. This put me in a precarious place and especially limited my endeavors since he was rarely willing to fund any request that benefited me. I was too outspoken and independent and this he detested. He punished me the only way he could—by not compensating me. My father would have been terribly angered and saddened by the vindictive nature of his brother's behavior.

I was determined that my brothers and sister would receive the best education we could afford. I fought hard for this, and Uncle Abraham made a nearly unbearable situation even more stressful. I was forced to put my long-dreamed plans to travel Europe to rest, not only due to finances but because I could not in good conscience leave my family now. They needed me in the absence of my father, and no one could have offered me anything to abandon them. Not only did Europe have to wait, but all of my aspirations had to shift. My immediate aim became supporting our household, now an issue of what I could earn. Not so much what I longed to do. Not what I believed was my purpose.

With my options limited as a woman, I fell into teaching. Ralph Waldo Emerson, or Waldo as I came to call him, informed me that Bronson Alcott was looking for a teacher for his Temple School in Boston. Elizabeth Peabody, who had held the position, was letting it go. Although it didn't pay a lot, it offered a new experience and some sort of income. Plus, I was drawn to working with Bronson, an on-and-off Concord inhabitant known for his progressive vision and approach to education.

Teaching offered me a platform to share and to mold beyond the tutoring I had previously done. Always a believer that if you have knowledge, share it with others, one way or another, teaching seemed the most direct way to do this. In this way, it held appeal, but I quickly discovered the enormous amount of preparation and tedium left me little time for my own endeavors.

To compensate for this, I rose early in the morning to work on my translation of a biography of Johann Wolfgang Goethe, the German creative I so deeply admired, and to fit in a walk, the fresh air and meditative quality of which I could not do without.

This grueling schedule, the fact that I was not being paid as promised, and the realization that Bronson's school was floundering due to controversy, convinced me to relinquish the position. What a relief! I could identify the aspects of teaching I valued and found much to feel good about there, but the drudgery and the energy it required weakened both my spirit and health.

Maria

We were fortunate to live in a spot that was central to all we needed— downtown, schools, and stores. It wasn't until high school that we needed to board a schoolbus.

Our summer walks to the playground were our most leisurely because it didn't matter when we arrived. Nok hockey and gimp crafting were always happening. We'd trudge along, the hot summer sun burning the tops of our heads. Sometimes we'd stop by the store that was in the front of a house to turn in glass Coke bottles for candy.

These walks were usually uneventful once we got past the house with the older guy who yelled terrifying versions of our names, "Ci-ci-cigarette and Maarrriiaa!" He was like Billy Goat Gruff and scared us with his big burly voice and rough mannerisms. Occasionally, he'd snatch one of us and throw us in the air, laughing, but we didn't laugh. We ran by as quickly as we could and turned the corner without looking back.

One day, almost to the little store, Theresa stepped on a piece of glass that cut right through her flimsy flip-flop, and the blood came fast. Panicking, we turned her around, tears streaming down her little cheeks, and hobbled her back home where Mom knew exactly what to do. Leaving her there, foot up with a band-aid, we hoofed it right back to the park. It was the happening place on these long summer days, with one activity being the plaster-of-Paris molds that, once dry and sanded soft, we painted in bright bold colors and carried home to show off.

I'm sure Mom welcomed us walking to the community playground, our independence giving her a temporary slice of her own.

Margaret

Outside, walking alone for my health and sanity, I could do nothing but that. I was free—free from routine, domestic details, mental work and toil, reading, translating, writing, and thinking, thinking, thinking in the mustiness of my room. It was time to spread my arms like the trees, to look up to the sky as the birds fly, to pick up my step as I would not do from room to room in the house. Time to breathe deeply and exhale loudly.

Walks I also relished with others, especially those I was in tune with, those with whom I was exploring not only the beckoning outdoors but the deeper thoughts dogging our minds. There were many paths to liberation and one of the most elevating was freedom from patterned thought—the freedom that came with questioning. Weighing ideas with another while walking in the company of what guides best, nature, was enlightening.

Although walks and talks around Cambridge with companions of the mind, walks and talks around Concord with those soaring in my direction, hours spent in the fresh air, and fresh minds were inspiring, walks alone along soft trails in the woods revived me best. What the softest breezes and shadiest spots had to impart, I heard as best I could.

People often described me as someone who ran on high energy, at a high speed, full throttle. My attraction to walks, the need to be outside, to be moving, even if the only place I was heading was eventually back home, may have helped to offset this. As it was, I often imploded, my head pounding, my body utterly exhausted. This walking practice of mine made it possible for me to last longer before being forced down for a few days and made to rest my active mind and my unending drive toward all.

Maria

OUR SCHOOL YEAR ALWAYS BEGAN WITH A CHURCH SERVICE attended by the students, their parents, and the teachers. While kneeling, we watched the teachers walk by on their way to communion. We didn't know who our teachers would be; this was long before the days of finding out before the school year began.

When an apparently new teacher with bleached blond hair and a striped micro-mini skirt passed by our pew, my mother whispered that she hoped none of us would have that woman as our teacher. But I did. Miss Katkin was my fourth-grade teacher.

What a school year it was. School as I knew it was tossed into the air. I'm not sure if this was a modern approach Miss Katkin employed—one radically different from what the nuns and veteran schoolteachers used—or if she had no plan in mind at all.

Before Miss Katkin, I never knew anything about my teachers' lives. But Miss Katkin shared everything with us. We knew about her boyfriend, Ricky; and her dog, Arrow. And that her parents owned a bakery in Portsmouth, two hours from Keene. On Mondays, Miss Katkin would often bring in cupcakes from the bakery—delectable cupcakes with little plastic decorations poking out of them. The routine and rote learning going on in the other classrooms couldn't compare with the thrill and excitement of what was going on in Miss Katkin's classroom.

Miss Katkin even went so far as to invite us to her apartment once so we could write on computer punch cards that she was our favorite teacher so she could be entered in the Favorite Teacher

Contest. A handful of us showed up at her place on a rainy Saturday morning. She gave us giant stacks of these cards and we wrote over and over again: Miss Katkin is our favorite teacher. She shuttled us popcorn and soda, and we marveled at her cool pad and petted Arrow when he came around. We were sad she didn't win.

Whatever her pedagogy, it wasn't working for me, and when test time came, I fumbled. Soon I received an academic warning, an official form stating that I wasn't performing well. My parents needed to sign this horrid piece of paper, and I was to return it on Monday. I'd been delivered to hell.

After school that Friday, I changed into my play clothes and folded the warning carefully, tucking it into my back pants pocket. At night I placed it under my pillow. This went on until Sunday night when I knew I had no choice but to present it to my parents. At that point, the piece of paper looked like it had been around forever, creased and crumpled.

When they saw it, my parents looked at one another. They spoke seriously to me about paying attention and trying harder. One of them signed the note, and I was so relieved I could have skipped away . . . but instead, walked sullenly.

I didn't get good grades from Miss Katkin, but even then I felt it was more her fault than mine. Whatever her grand plan was, it was falling flat with me. But I learned that year. I learned about the glamour of a life of dating, having a career, and living in an apartment—a different existence for a young woman than I had seen in real life.

With the signed warning in my bag, I was ready for Monday, hoping for cupcakes. Miss Katkin was my favorite teacher.

Margaret

Not long after I left Bronson Alcott's Temple School, I was offered another teaching position at Greene Street School in Providence, Rhode Island. The pay was much better and I was guaranteed to receive it. I had to put my family's financial needs first, and this salary would ease a lot of our worries and assist in putting my brothers through Harvard. It would require living away, but with the ages my siblings were now, my mother would be able to manage all right without me being there day to day. Hoping this position would be less exhausting, I accepted it.

Indeed, this position turned out to be much more rewarding than the first, and being paid as promised made the task even more tolerable. Although I was exacting and came down hard on my students—all females—ultimately, they responded with the courage and focus I expected of them and knew they possessed.

I demanded that they think as well as study; that they talk as well as recite. We bonded around the constant quest toward perfection, not settling for mediocrity, not allowing ourselves to do less than we were capable of doing. This drive and the results of it kept me afloat most days. It kept them afloat as well and they felt motivated and empowered.

I recall a day I came down particularly hard on a fledging student, calling her out for not working to capacity and reminding her that this approach would not serve her well. Some hours later, a posse of this girl's friends approached and asked to have a word. They eloquently and vehemently defended their friend's solid nature and tendency toward hard work. They explained they were speaking on her behalf because she was too upset to do it for herself. I realized then that I might have crushed a fragile soul and applauded her friends for stepping up on her behalf. I explained my motive as an attempt to startle and motivate and apologized for the misstep.

In a huddle, we laughed and hugged, and I believe a tear or two may have been shed. We bonded as those on a joint mission are wont to do. This is but an example of the mutual growth and trust established between my students and me while at Greene Street School.

Once again unwilling to give up my translating and writing projects, I rose early to sustain progress and spent the rest of the day giving what I had left to my pupils. Whenever possible, I continued with my own needs later in the day as well as spending many an evening in the company of the cultural and societal scene in Providence. I began to wear thin and to feel the effects on my physical health. It was clear I could not keep this up for much longer and after two years of satisfying teaching, I resigned and trusted that I would find a way to continue as the dutiful oldest daughter and big sister, yet somehow be true to the nature of myself.

A crown of duties, both large and small, I donned for being firstborn and female, and this made me who I was, strength and confidence major fibers of my being.

Maria

SUNDAYS WERE FAMILY DAYS WHEN WE WERE GROWING UP. Even as teens, we were expected to be home with the family on Sunday. What might be viewed by some as torture was actually a godsend. Sunday was a sanctuary day—a safe and comfortable day protected from the often stressful and heightened energy of the weekdays, especially Fridays and Saturdays. Those days were fighting days, days when you vied for position with your friends and peers. Those were days you were put to the wolves, in a way. Friday and Saturday nights presented social jousting, both titillating and terrifying.

But Sunday . . .

When we were young, we attended the 12:15 p.m. Mass, all eight of us filing down the aisle, most weeks late. We would be ready and waiting, waiting for Dad to emerge from the bathroom. When we heard that door creak, we grabbed our jackets and headed for the station wagon. We did a lot of waiting as children. Whether it was in the car while our parents grocery shopped or in the car while Dad had one more drink with his cronies at the club, we waited. Some of our most creative play transpired while confined to the car, along with some of our most potent squabbles, especially when one kid's sweaty skin stuck to another kid's sweaty skin. Often there was not enough air to breathe, even in a station wagon as big as ours—a real boat— with all the windows down.

Waiting for church though, we'd gather in the living room to watch *Community Auditions*, broadcast from Boston. There were five contestants on this local show, all about our ages, and we'd each pair up with one. My oldest sister would align with number one, and then on down the line. David, the youngest of six, had to claim last week's winner called back to receive their star. That basically left him out, but he was used to that and pretty good-natured about his position in the clan. We'd jeer at each other's contestants and boast loudly about our own if they were especially good that week. Our antics were soon usurped by a rote Catholic Mass that was rarely under an hour long in those days.

Released from church, we'd pick up the Sunday paper, and the long, leisurely afternoon loomed. We'd occupy ourselves with a variety of activities. Sometimes that would be homework, especially as we got older and homework became more regularly assigned and critical. We'd circulate the funnies or comics printed in color in the Sunday paper, laughing at Dagwood or an especially relevant "Family Circus." Sometimes we'd take Silly Putty to the funnies, imprinting Beetle Bailey's face and stretching it to all sorts of strange dimensions.

Most often we would trade our church clothes for play clothes and spend the afternoon outside. When we got a little older, our mother would let us walk to Adams Drugstore with our nickels and dimes to buy candy after dinner. We'd take our time, weaving through the fields on well-worn paths with pieces of long grass waving in our teeth. Once under the bright lights of the store, we'd take what seemed hours deciding which candy we wanted, never having quite enough money to buy our first choice and refusing to pool our money because we had to pool everything else.

Sundays were so laid back that I even taught myself how to blow a bubble with bubble gum one Sunday afternoon. Alone in the living room, slowly rocking in the rocking chair, I tried over and over again, maneuvering the wad between my tongue and teeth, until, by Jesus, I did it!

Sunday was the day my father cooked, the smell of rich spaghetti sauce making our mouths water for hours. He and my mother spent the better part of the afternoon in the kitchen cooking and reading the paper, passing the funnies off to us when they were finished, of course.

As teens, we four girls joined the church folk group and sang at the 9:30 a.m. Mass. For this Mass, we were never late. I relished that hour at the front of the church to the right of the altar. The songs we sang were mostly beautiful and meaningful and our heavenly harmonies made me tingle inside. Folk group introduced a social side to church, which, as teens, was welcomed. Often my boyfriend would be in one of the front pews with his family at this Mass. But on Sunday, I returned home with my sisters. Boyfriends were not invited.

Margaret

It was a gorgeous Sunday afternoon, and I was staying with the Emersons in Concord for a stretch. I decided to take a walk and wandered my way through town and into the woods, finally coming to a grassy opening near Sleepy Hollow. There I sat myself on the soft green expanse in the sunshine, completely at ease with all, nothing between me and the hospitable earth.

Enjoying the brightest hues and freshest air, I spotted a lone figure emerging from the woods.

It didn't take long for me to recognize Nathaniel Hawthorne on his way to Emerson's to return a book I had left at his house the day before. His approach cast a shadow, but I didn't mind. As usual, we engaged in easy conversation and soon he sat beside me. There was much to talk and laugh about. He explained that his wife, Sophia, was home with one of her sisters who had come by for a visit.

Conversing with Nathaniel resembled connecting with a boy on the precipice of becoming a man. Nathaniel—one foot in the past, the other in the future—struggled to soundly navigate the present, portraying one way of life, secretly desiring another. It struck me as though the window to change was open, allowing for fresh air, but the door was bolted, not allowing complete passage. How awful, the pull of potentiality so strong but the chains of fear stronger. Could any one of us help release him? His writings often revealed this conflict but seemed to do little to free him.

But that Sunday afternoon was memorable, encompassed by gentle air and the freedom of outdoor talk. Soon another figure emerged—my host, Waldo. He enthusiastically joined us and as the sun began to set, the three of us continued to exchange some most fascinating thoughts, my earlier musings enhanced, not derailed in any way—always a concern when precious solitude is invaded.

What richness on a wide-open Sunday afternoon. When the light began to fade, Waldo and I made our way back to his residence and Hawthorne to his, where Sophia and her sister awaited. These impromptu meetings of the minds and hearts, running into neighbors and taking the time to connect in ways busy lives did not often permit, nourished my soul. I couldn't be in better company than with those who lived in the town of Concord, Massachusetts.

Back at the Emersons, once supper was over, I settled into the room across the hall from Waldo's study, my workspace while I was there. Knowing Waldo was nearby engaged in the same was comforting and inspiring. I would pick up reading where I left off or work on my writing. Or, as I did almost daily, write a letter to a dear friend or family member. Those days in Concord with the Emersons and others were some of the very best.

Maria

My sister shouted from the kitchen, "Maria, look what was delivered for you!" We locked eyes as she handed me the bouquet. Being a junior and senior in high school, a dozen red roses delivered to the door had real juicy potential. Fumbling, I removed the tiny card from its tiny envelope and read it in disbelief. Evan? The guy who imitated my lisp in class? The guy who was pretty much the clown among his friends? HE sent me a dozen red roses?

The look of utter disappointment on my sister's face reflected that of my own. While arranging the red gems in a vase, I so wished they were from someone else. There were plenty of other guys who, had they sent this bouquet, my sister and I would be clasping each other's forearms, jumping up and down, mercilessly screaming.

Instead, I was left to wonder why someone who made fun of me in front of the entire class, especially a public-speaking class, would do something like this. I guess I didn't realize that he liked me. I don't remember whether I acknowledged this gesture or not. It would have been my style then to not say anything, to ignore him as much as possible and to blush when he looked my way or addressed me. You know those games.

Months later, a bunch of friends and I ended up at Evan's house. It was a dark, rainy night as we approached the sprawling ranch with the attached garage, an unusual build in this small New England town. Once in the house, we were greeted by two graceful Weimaraner dogs that Evan quickly escorted away. We settled into our usual antics, talking, joking, listening to Supertramp, and drinking. Evan was playing host and paying a lot of attention to me. I had to admit, although I had no interest in him as someone I would go out with, the attention was flattering and fun.

The scene was suddenly shattered when Dan ran in shouting that one of the dogs had been hit in the road. Everything was suspended. Evan and a couple others raced outside. A few of us hung back, pressing the palms of our hands against our cheeks, terrified. Someone sprinted back in yelling for a blanket. They were going to rush the dog to the vet.

To escape the chaos, I stepped out into the garage where, surprisingly, I encountered Evan crying. He was trying to compose himself, he said. I approached him to tell him how sorry I was and how awful I felt. He turned to me, wiping tears from his cheeks and moved closer, close enough where I could feel his breath. I asked if there was anything I could do, and he said yes, I could kiss him. I was shocked that he would think of such a thing while in such grief. But I said yes and kissed him.

The beautiful dog didn't survive, and I forever felt sad and guilty about that.

When Evan imitated my lisp in class, I turned away, hoping someone would change the subject and we'd move on from that awful feeling of being made fun of. I remember my mother always said that if someone was mean to you, it was probably because they liked you. I had mixed feelings about that sentiment, but here, I supposed it may have been true. Maybe, I wondered, he thought by putting me down he would make me sound less desirable to others so he'd stand a better chance with me. Maybe.

Margaret

BEING PRIMARILY HOME SCHOOLED, AND YEARS AHEAD OF my siblings, I absorbed everything like a sponge and reached out to grasp even more. I had received about as much adult attention as a child could take. Instead of being overwhelmed by this, I gathered the courage to meet it head-on, and once I had conquered that, I would never back down from anything.

Being the constant recipient of such attention, it was something I grew to desire. Without it, I felt isolated, incomplete. Some of my friends would comment about my need for attention. I was not ashamed of my occasional neediness. It only showed how intensely I craved meaningful connections in a world more comfortable with surface encounters, a world more concerned about what it looked like than what it was.

I got after Waldo about this once, and some misinterpreted my motive as wanting more than a friendship with him. What I wanted was a more intimate friendship, one of the heart as well as the mind, as I did with all my good friends. Waldo was a man of the head, floating above this earthly plane. I longed to bring him down some and have him open up and share more of his humanness with those around him, not interact only as he would with his readers and audiences.

I discovered that perhaps it was not in him to connect in this way—to anyone, not only me. I would not have come between him and his wife, Lidian, although I fear my relations with Waldo did not make her role as his wife any easier. I had my relationship with Lidian, too, as well as their son, little Waldo, whom I loved with the entirety of my heart.

Yes, I did have a distinct desire for attention. Being as intense as I was rendered me ravenous for authentic human interaction. This, balanced with clean solitude, reading, thinking, writing, and hours of walking and sitting with nature, offered me what felt like a direct connection with the universe.

Maria

I'D ALWAYS LOVED THE MONTH AND DATE OF MY BIRTHDAY. It seemed to me the best birthday ever—a sweet-smelling month, May, and a balanced, even number, twenty-two. Nothing ever suited me more naturally than my birthday, and I imagined that was how the universe operated. I often wondered if others felt this way about their birthday month and day. I hoped so because it offered an annual sense of well-being and joy. I imagined that when or if I ever turned 100, my birthday details would still warm my heart.

May is especially treasured in New England. After long winters, the lilacs and lily-of-the valley, the scents of the budding spring, are greedily inhaled. Two of my favorites, Aunt Caroline and Gram, always thought my birthday was the twenty-first. The white station wagon would make its way down our dead-end street and slowly crunch on the gravel driveway. That's when my mother would announce, again, that they thought it was my birthday today, not tomorrow. They'd make their way out of the car with lily-of-the-valley in a small vase, a saran-covered homemade sponge cake, and a bag full of beautifully wrapped and ribboned gifts.

Magically, the kitchen table became a warm and generous hearth of love and doting. These two women made me feel more loved than any other people in the world could. I wasn't as wild about the sponge cake as others were, but in those moments, I let the soft, lemony sponge just melt on my tongue and sipped the freshly brewed coffee with complete joy, the potent scent of the lily-of-the-valley mixing in. I was intoxicated. Slowly, I'd open Aunt Caroline's artistically wrapped gifts, folding up the paper as I went (because you did not ball up her special wrapping paper and whip it at your brother). I'd relish the small gifts she offered, things you would never need or ever buy for yourself; but such intricate treasures would be forever cherished and Aunt Caroline would be forever remembered for giving them to you.

Time seemed to stand still around the kitchen table the day before my birthday. I was enveloped and snuggled in love and attention, as I'm sure I was on the day I was born. They gave me a remarkable gift by stretching out my birthday; they gifted me with an extra day of love and attention. I wish I had thanked them for that; I wish I had let them know that their visits the day before my birthday meant so much.

Margaret

OH, THAT TIME OF YEAR WHEN YOU CAN LEAVE THE windows open a bit, let the young spring air waft in, and hear the birds in a springtime frenzy. My birthday being the twenty-third of May made for a bright occasion most years.

One year I was given a gift of the greatest proportions: another baby brother my parents named Edward. My birthday was never my own again from that year on. Mother handed him to me and told me since he was born on my birthday, he was naturally very much mine. She was overwhelmed with the rest of the children, so she wasn't entirely untruthful with this proclamation.

As I held newborn Edward in my arms, many feelings coursed through my veins. I was already saddled with the domestic chores around the house and charged with tutoring my younger brothers and sister. Now this innocent little bundle handed to me on my eighteenth birthday became another player in the conspiracy to rob me of my life. But how could I not naturally love this beautiful baby? I immediately felt a connection and would work him into my daily existence as I had all the other duties and roles.

As a year passed and the spring and summer months unfolded once again, little Edward became sick. It was obvious to us that he was not himself and was becoming weaker and weaker with each passing day. There was not anything to be done, we were told, but to keep him comfortable and to pray for his healing from whatever disease had captivated his perfect little body. I held Edward close to my chest for weeks, rocking him and breathing into his warm little neck. Please do not take this gift from me. Please let Edward grow and blossom. But it was not to be and this sweet baby brother passed away in my arms, bringing back all the memories of losing my little sister, Julia Adelaide.

My birthday was never the same from the day Edward was born on it, only to live a little over a year. Every May 23 from that time on was a melancholic reminder of the powerlessness to save this baby, my youngest brother, Edward.

Yet I would be untruthful if I didn't confess that when he passed in my arms, I witnessed the peace he was inheriting at that moment, and the beauty of that new existence was evident all around me, especially in Edward's angelic face.

In later years, I worked it so that my birthday was the day I completed writing projects, one being my book, *Summer on the Lakes*, in 1843. Knowing it was a meaningful day for so many reasons, it seemed fitting to gift myself by completing something monumental.

It so happens that years later my sister Ellen birthed her baby girl on May 23 and named her after me. She was called Greta.

Maria

Our junior high school was downtown where the railroad tracks rambled. We followed them, listening and looking for trains as we balanced on the rails and picked up the loose railroad spikes randomly lying around, rusty and tired. I never understood how they came to just lie there for the taking, but there they were, like fallen apples, overripe and needy.

On one side of the tracks was Gilbo Avenue, a busy curved road. On the other was Central Screw, where, yes, they manufactured screws. There was no air conditioning in that large building, so in the spring and summer the windows would be open, and some of the men would whistle at us as we walked by on the tracks. That creeped us out. They looked old and like prisoners to us. One day, my friend Luanna stopped and scrawled a note: *Take a picture, it lasts longer!* Darting up to one of the windowsills, she set it there and we ran away laughing, tripping over the railroad ties, thinking we were so clever.

I never felt unsafe, even with these men hanging out the windows catcalling at us because my Uncle Herbie worked there. It seemed that he'd protect us; he'd admonish his co-workers, telling them, "Those are my nieces and their friends, so back off." But I didn't know where in the building Uncle Herbie worked, and if he was at a window, would he have said anything at all?

Walks home were always more enjoyable than the walks to school, of course. We were free to goof off and meander, both physically and mentally. Our laughs were louder, our exchanges bolder. We had survived another day of junior high and that was something, really something.

Margaret

I HAD WALKING ROUTES IN CAMBRIDGE, BOSTON, GROTON, Providence, and finally in New York City, where my walks to and from the omnibus to the house were by far the most peaceful moments of my day.

It was quite a distance from the street to the house, the path well-worn and winding, and because I was usually by myself either beginning or ending my day, it became a ritual: In the mornings, the birds and small creatures were in high gear, often forcing me to stop and consider their busyness; joy and survival mixed in a graceful way. This brought a smile to my face most mornings. The sun beaming through branches and bushes, creating a shifting mosaic on the hard-packed dirt, the fragrance of flowers and plant life, arresting and often amazingly reminiscent. Once out onto the street, my workday began, me readier to manage it with the serenity of my stroll. I'd chuckle at myself, the way I'd cock my head this way and that looking for the bus. How like a bird I must have appeared!

Walking the busy streets of the city continually played with my thoughts and emotions. At times, I felt blessed to be one of the masses, the great machine of the city, of modern life, each person contributing in their way, from those in their aprons sweeping their store entrances to those in their suits climbing the stairs to their law offices. Me, eyes wide open as a journalist must, seeing too much of what was shameful and sad, those visibly downtrodden and aimless. The longing in the eyes of men, women, and children, immigrants and homeless on the streets. Pressing on me daily was the need for various kinds of social reform and there was no doubt of what we were capable of, if a priority, and in a country such as ours, it needed to be.

At last, I'd climb the stairs in the Tribune building, situate myself at my desk, my head swimming with too much and oh, all the work to be done.

Maria

SIXTH GRADE WAS A MIXED BAG OF EXPERIENCES. SOMEHOW, I was Dorothy in *The Wizard of Oz* and delivered "Somewhere Over the Rainbow" alone on stage with a stuffed animal under my arm as Toto. I must have had a decent voice, or I doubt the Glee Club teacher would have cast me in the role. Plus, all the backyard plays my sister cast me in growing up had prepared me well. I was good at memorizing lines and belting out a song.

The evening of the show, freshly bathed and in our bathrobes, my younger sister, Glinda the Good Witch, and I attempted to eat dinner before being driven to the auditorium. I pushed pieces of hot dog around on my plate and nibbled a couple kernels of corn, too nervous to eat. That night we didn't have to clear our plates.

I have no detailed recollection of the performance, but a couple of photos my father snapped focused on the elevated stage and made me look very tall with long stick legs—giant-like and steady. I didn't wear the usual blue gingham of Dorothy, and the ruby slippers were patchwork shoes in shades of mauve that I happened to own. Clearly, there was no costume budget. But we pulled it off, our teacher satisfied with the performance, our families proud.

St. Joseph's, the one Catholic school in town, went through the sixth grade, which was a curse when we moved on to junior high school. The public schools went through fifth grade, and from there, students transitioned into junior high for grade six—. everyone except those of us at St. Joe's. We came into the junior high at the start of seventh grade when the peer groups were already formed and everyone knew how to work the combination locks on their lockers and could find their way around the building without getting kissed or kicked by Mrs. Woodward. They already had someone to sit with in the jungle of the cafeteria. We St. Joe's students were at a serious disadvantage.

As a result, the confidence I had built up in sixth grade seemed to shrink in the face of the hard, cruel world of junior high. I had but a few friends, maybe two good ones and another I could eat lunch with, at least. Although not my best years, I survived the intense awkwardness, along with many others who roamed the halls shrouded in a new brand of insecurity.

Margaret

My parents, so sure and proud of who I was before, started to almost panic about what my future had in store. When they initially enrolled me in the Cambridge Port School—a private grammar school—at age nine, they hoped, along with a healthy dose of academics, that I would develop socially, that my association with other girls my age would help shape me and instruct me in the ways of being a proper girl.

I did develop some friendships with a couple of the girls in my class and that was good enough, in my estimation. Most of the boys in the class opposite ours saw me as a curiosity—an oddity, smart but weird. I was certainly not the typical female specimen, in brains or body. It was almost as though my advanced knowledge from all the instruction I had endured and all the reading I did sped up my physical development, causing me to be bigger for my age, as well as smarter.

But it didn't end with the boys discounting me. The girls didn't view me as one of them either. From there, relations with the girls not only didn't develop but there was some hostility, and when my parents caught wind of it, they pulled me from Port School, feeling it wasn't serving the purposes they had hoped it would.

My parents again struggled with where to place me, frantically trying to come up with the best option to meet all needs. Against my mother's wishes, and along with some persuading on my part, my father decided to send me to Dr. Park's Boston Lyceum, which was known then as offering the most rigorous academics for girls. Once again, the hope was that, along with academics, I'd be socialized in ways that would prepare me for the life a young woman could expect to lead in the rigid sphere of domesticity.

Eventually, I departed this school as well, which wasn't my choice. But as children, those choices usually are not ours. Although, it was my decision to throw a dance party for myself and all the girls I knew. I figured that although not many of them cared for me, an invitation to a dance party would be difficult to pass up. It would be a chance to say goodbye as well as feel like I did belong in some way and, hopefully, I would exit on a higher note.

My father was away in Washington, but he approved my plan and my mother set forth to coordinate the event. Two of my father's brothers also helped, hiring the musicians and assisting with other arrangements. I told my father I would invite forty girlfriends, but I invited ninety—all the girls I knew in my neighborhood, and girls from Port School in Cambridge as well as Dr. Park's. I cast the net far and wide, hoping to initiate a gala that would inject me with a sense of great excitement, rosy my cheeks a bit, and offer me hope that I was not too much of an oddity, an outcast, but that I did fit in when the occasion called for it.

My imagination ran wild with the vision of such a lively and noteworthy gathering but only nine girls responded that they would attend. That was indeed the number of girls who showed up on that snowy night to join the festivities at our grand house in Boston. I pretended that it was all right and that it was the snow that had kept so many others from attending. Inside, I was not surprised. Admittedly, a slice of me was stung and saddened, yet I was fortunate then and always for the constant fire burning in me, the confidence and hope that would always fuel me forward. My favorite gem, the red carbuncle, that fiery jewel burning steady, would remind me and rescue me from the more mundane, disappointing strictures of human society.

In retrospect, I was thankful that the gathering didn't manifest in the way I had feverishly imagined. If it had been a well-attended, magnificent event, perhaps I would have had to extricate myself from such an energy-robbing existence, a typically devoid platform. Instead, the shallow thrill never welcomed me, and for this, I felt almost blessed. My mother's only remark to my father's inquiry about the dance party was that she was glad it was over and no one spoke of it again.

From there, I was sent to another school, Miss Prescott's Young Ladies' Seminary, where fitting in went from bad to worse. Considering it was not my deep desire to assimilate, to absorb the ways of society, especially ways for women, I was able to experience some of my mistreatment as an out-of-body experience and write about it in a detached, fictional way. I created a drama for myself that stoked passion instead of hurt, a story of rescue and redemption. I emerged from my experience at this school intact, with a lifelong friendship with Miss Prescott herself and secure in the knowledge that although I was considered ugly and odd by many, I would always be smart and ambitious.

TWO

Maria

We were sheltered growing up. Our world revolved around our home on Hooper St., then rippled to our schools, church, and the small town of Keene, New Hampshire. My parents didn't subscribe to any other newspaper than the local one and we rarely watched the news on television. I don't recall my parents discussing politics or national and world affairs at the table. Maybe on Sundays at my grandparents' house, after dinner when all the adults would sit around sipping wine and coffee, maybe I heard bits and pieces as I ran through the crowded dining room in pursuit of a cousin, but being young, I never stopped long enough to listen.

The monthly National Geographic and our World Book Encyclopedia set were my means to peek at the rest of the world. And, of course, whatever we covered in our dusty textbooks at school. I would sit on the living room rug staring at images of starving children in Africa or of colorfully dressed people along a river somewhere in India. In high school, I still didn't tune in. One of my older sisters, Laura, did watch the news and I remember her on the couch one day, slapping her thigh and chanting along with some far away demonstration, "Kill Kissinger, kill Kissinger!" and I giggled at the sight, no idea or interest about the context of the segment.

When I first moved to Cambridge for college, and then New York City for summers, I was surprised by the people living on the street. I knew they were probably hungry and the look in their eyes conveyed an anger and desperation that frightened me. I rarely gave them anything but my sister, Cecilia, always handed them something, sometimes a twenty-dollar bill if that's all she had on her.

It amazes and dismays me to think how ignorant I was, my exposure so limited. In a small, New England town at that time, I suppose it wasn't that unusual. Others may have been exposed to more, the *New York Times* or *Boston Globe* delivered to their doors, parents tuned in to the news and discussing politics and world events at the dinner table, travel outside of one's state and country. It certainly wasn't that nothing was going on in the sixties and seventies. But I suppose in some ways, ignorance was indeed bliss, while it lasted.

On a kibbutz in Israel years later, this ignorance would confirm for many of my international friends just how clueless many Americans were when it came to even their own politics and their country's posture in the world. My kibbutz friends from Ireland, England, Denmark, Germany, Zimbabwe, Australia, and more would talk circles around me and knew so much more than I did about my own country. It was a humbling and embarrassing situation, and the fact that they were not surprised by it made me feel even more predictable. How could I be so out of touch? How could I live in such a powerful country and know so little? Why didn't they teach me anything? And the bigger question was: why didn't I care?

I had been raised to believe I was an Italian American, my grandparents having come from Italy and my dad being a first-generation American. I was proud of my Italian heritage, even though I was only half Italian. But on the kibbutz, sitting on the veranda of our volunteer hut in the Negev Desert with these young people from all over the world, I was American through and through, not a speck Italian. And it wasn't a good feeling. I vowed I would change, I would become knowledgeable, and I would read up on current events, politics, economics, and more. I decided it was time to care.

Margaret

BEING HEAVILY STEEPED IN THE CLASSICS COULD NOT HELP but set me on an earnest quest for truth, beauty, and, I hoped, immortality! Later, considered the most intelligent woman in America, I garnered recognition along with ridicule and disdain. I persevered and with the foothold of a few fair and open-minded men and like-minded women, I scrambled as far as I could, much further than most. Ralph Waldo Emerson and others selected me as the first editor of *The Dial*, and after reading my travelogue, *Summer on the Lakes*, in 1843, Horace Greeley offered me a position with the *New York Tribune*, one that provided an opportunity to explore new environs in New York and ultimately abroad.

Although not allowed to enroll, I became friend and confidante to many of the students and graduates of Harvard College and was the first woman allowed in their library to conduct research. The looks I endured ranged from shock to abhorrence, but I did my work regardless. I forged ahead. I did not have a choice, truly, for I knew I was as smart, as talented, as interesting, as ambitious, and as worthy as any man.

All along, I harbored concerns about being discounted. I knew there were those who didn't approve, who wanted to see me fail, and those who pitied me. I worried my accomplishments would be buried, and I would be permanently silenced when I died, even by those I counted as friends, those who recognized and valued my contributions. But I feared I would be especially discounted by those who made no secret of their distaste for me when I was alive, believing I was out of bounds and thought too highly of myself.

There were those who bitterly dubbed me Queen Margaret, but I say with so many kings, ought not there be as many queens? And those who mocked my "Let them be sea captains," but why not? I believed there should be no limit on the choices for women except their own desires. Women sea captains should reap as much satisfaction and praise as their male counterparts for a job well done, don't you think?

Early on I was aware that who I was and what I did mattered, not only for me but for others; that what I stood for would continue to be relevant and necessary; that who I was and how I lived would continue to inspire. It was clear to me that many of my male contemporaries—Ralph Waldo Emerson, Henry David Thoreau, Nathaniel Hawthorne, and Edgar Allan Poe, to name a few—would be remembered in big ways, and rightly so, but my place would be obscured. That was unfair and detrimental, especially for women.

For that I could not stand.

Maria

I'M PRETTY SURE IT WAS MY HIGH SCHOOL GUIDANCE counselor who suggested Lesley College. I recall it wasn't wholeheartedly recommended since it was such a pricey school in Cambridge, Massachusetts, but since I had mentioned an interest in being an elementary schoolteacher, it must have come up in one of our meetings. And it stuck. No, I wasn't interested in the college in my hometown. I wanted to get out of Keene.

I plunged into my college career with enthusiasm and focus. Lesley College, then a women's school, and me wanting to study elementary education, which Lesley was known for, seemed an ideal match. From the start, I felt like I belonged there. Being a very small school, I found my place readily. Only two hours from my home in New Hampshire and a desirable place for others to visit, I was well positioned. I felt motivated to do well in my courses and to move steadily forward in this new phase of my life.

I fell in love with bustling Cambridge, strolling down Mass. Ave., often by myself, stopping in the boutiques and checking out the quaint cafés. I remember saving my meager earnings from my work-study job in the college library to buy a sweater I coveted in one of the shop windows. I wore that sweater for years—one of the first pieces of clothing I owned that didn't involve sisters borrowing it on a regular basis. This shoulder-padded, bright-pink sweater was a good color for me and was distinctly mine.

I loved walking through Harvard Yard, the majestic gates and arches, and stepping into Harvard Square. I enjoyed the crisp fall days strolling along the Charles River, the crew teams effortlessly skirting up and down with speed and grace. People would whip by me running or on roller skates or bicycles. I loved going into the Harvard Coop and browsing the books and Harvard apparel. Yes, even though we went to Lesley, my friends and I wore more Harvard gear than Lesley, and on the weekends, we spent more time on the Harvard and MIT campuses than we did our own.

The first day I was bused to a kindergarten class in Framingham during my second semester at Lesley was the day I realized I did not want to be an elementary school teacher. It hit me strong and clear. This was not for me. It appeared I would need to leave my beloved Lesley College and Cambridge behind since the school didn't offer many other options—or at least, any I was interested in.

My departure from Lesley to the University of New Hampshire was one of the darkest turns I'd ever take. Going from a place where I felt grounded and purposeful and tumbling into an abyss of the unknown, I latched onto two of my sisters and their lives, sometimes resenting their attempts to help.

Perhaps I was destined to fall at some point anyway and instead of citing my sisters in some twisted way as abettors to my suffering, I now credit them with lending me a hand when I needed it most.

Margaret

I TAUGHT MYSELF LATIN, GREEK, GERMAN, AND FINALLY, French and Italian. I was a worldly and inquisitive person from a young age due to the extensive reading and learning my father had assigned. As a result, I had a firm grasp on history, politics, literature, and art, along with a fresh vision for the future. I became adept at sharing my thoughts and knowledge and believed this was important. Although some called me arrogant, I did not feel superior. I only wanted to claim my space in a world of male dominance, a roomful of men, and if I were to pretend and play modest as though I didn't know as much or wasn't as capable as I was, I would not have been able to do everything I did. My intention was not to make anyone feel bad or less; I was only determined to not lower myself to make them feel good. Instead, I believed they should lift themselves up, which is how I lived my days, always striving to become wiser and closer to perfect.

My aim was to speak my truth and to empower and enlighten others, especially women. As I moved forward, creating and seizing opportunities, I had a vision for our country that truly embraced the ideals of freedom and justice for all. Years later while in Rome, I composed columns for the *Tribune* to keep my country informed and to illuminate the vital importance of independence. I lived among the battle and worked in the military hospital to keep the wounded and dying as comfortable and hopeful as possible, I was desperate to see freedom prevail. It wasn't to be for Italy then, but I vowed to never stop fighting for it, everywhere.

In big and small ways, I was misunderstood. Being a woman, I was easy prey for my looks. I did have some curvature of the spine that caused my neck to protrude. Some said this characteristic resembled a swan, others labeled it freakish. I could not see well and often squinted and batted my tired eyes. Some noted my dancing gray eyes, others labeled my squinting as snobbery.

One of my acquaintances, angry at me for what he perceived as me being a busybody, allowed publication of a terribly unflattering caricature of me in his paper. It was ironic because he had his own unique look: a large forehead and hair that could not be tamed. Yes, Mr. Poe, when you went low, I let you go. Our lives crossed paths as journalists, and we often met at literary gatherings in New York City. We thought highly of one another's works and were honest and fair in our critiques, and we were known to tease one another, which our readers found amusing.

Mr. Poe is rumored to have said—*Humanity is divided into men, women, and Margaret Fuller*—which was always open for interpretation, but I chose to take it as a compliment, for I didn't fit either silo. Or perhaps I fit both better than most.

Maria

I HAD HIT BOTTOM. EVEN THE ROOM I WAS LIVING IN OFF-campus was in the basement. I couldn't complain. I didn't have any friends of my own and was fortunate my sister and her boyfriend offered to have me live with them and three other guys on Young Drive. All the bedrooms were spoken for, so I got the basement. It was actually ideal since all I felt like doing was burrowing.

It was spring semester and why they called it that was beyond me. It should have been called the "dreadfully cold semester" since it ended in early May when spring was just arriving in New Hampshire. Being so cold gave me even more hiding opportunity—in a big, long coat my sister Cecilia handed down to me. It was labeled my "Hogan" coat since it looked like something right out of *Hogan's Heroes*.

I was a ball of confusion and anger that cold semester, in that coat, sleeping in that basement. Everything I was and thought I wanted was gone. I was the pretty one, right? I was thin and popular and caused no trouble. Now I was heavier and a little fish in a big pond, other attractive young women trampling me at every turn. I longed to return to my old self but I could not muster up the motivation. Instead, I entered the wrestling ring with food, and it became my focus and archenemy.

I had believed I wanted elementary education. Every time my dad introduced me to someone—long-lost relatives and friends of his at the club—he always reinforced this: "This is Maria. She's going to be an elementary school teacher." All would applaud. What a great thing to be! Now knowing I did not want it, I faced a void. I tried psychology, thinking I might want to be a child psychologist. That didn't stick.

Theresa's boyfriend tried to help. He'd counsel me at the kitchen table every Tuesday morning as neither of us had class until later. He tried to get me to see that the world was my oyster, that I could do anything I wanted, that I should enjoy what was in front of me, as he did. No one enjoyed their food and coffee more than Yoni. Yoni had already served in the Israeli army, traveled Europe, and driven across the US on his motorcycle. I listened to him, and he usually made me feel better, temporarily. But then I'd slip back into my darkness, my room in the basement, my Hogan coat that clung a little too tightly around my ankles when I tried to pick up my pace.

I had no sense of humor. When my sister said something to me in jest one morning while we were walking to a class we had together, I threw my coffee on the ground and stomped off as best I could in my Hogan, skipping class and leaving her to worry. My little sister, the girl who would stay home and sew on a Saturday night in high school, was light years ahead of me.

That political science class, the one I had with Theresa, was my lowest grade ever. Yes, the instructor was attractive and drove an MG. That was intriguing. But the material just didn't sink in. I remember my grade was wavering, needing rescue. Theresa and I were in her room studying for the final, but I curled up in the fetal position on her bed and went to sleep.

Margaret

I HAVE HAD A SOLID SENSE OF SELF SINCE THE DAY I STOPPED mid-skip and asked myself, Who is this Margaret Fuller? And knew I had the answer. Even when, as a child, I decided I would be called by my middle name, Margaret, and not my first name, Sarah, my parents had to accept that because it would be no other way.

When I read or overheard hurtful, negative comments, it stung. But I was determined not to let this knock me down. I diffused these comments by putting them in context and turning them over in my head a bit, considering from where they came and why. A couple of times I wrote about upsetting situations in a masked way. People closest to me could detect that the stories were not entirely fictional, and one situation got me into a bit of trouble. Yet, reworking a hurtful situation allowed me the power to make it what I wanted it to be and to leave it behind more readily.

I guess you could say I had a tough skin and was determined to become the best person I could be, and to that end, I worked to not expend unnecessary energy in any other direction whenever possible. But at times, the pull on my heart was strong and would weigh me down, forcing me to question whether I could take another step forward.

I always knew the answer.

Maria

THIS IS JUST A SHELL, JUST A SHELL, MY DAD WOULD SAY, poking his finger into my arm. He'd do this when I was fretting about what I looked like. He'd do it when he saw I was being overly vain, lamenting my hair, my clothes, or an unfortunate pimple on my face. Yeah, it was a shell, but I had learned it was important. Instead of protecting as shells normally do, it delivered great struggle and vulnerability.

My sister Theresa was more outspoken, less afraid to say what she thought, what she believed. Sometimes she would wear a pin with Fozzie Bear on it that read, Exercise Your Right to Goof Off. She didn't goof off all the time though. She knew when to be serious and how to be a true friend. And for all of this she paid. Theresa was nicknamed Poodle by many of her female peers who didn't like what they saw. They called her Poodle because of her perm, the forced curls burned into her long blond hair.

I became known to them as Poodle's Sister. We laughed it off. We had our own names for them, especially their ringleader. There was the occasional physical fight between the Poodle posse and her rivals, but I was not involved to that degree.

Honestly, I didn't have the courage to swing a punch—or my Candie's high heels, as my sister had done—at anyone.

Margaret

THE EXPECTATIONS MY FATHER HAD FOR ME WERE tremendous. I saw no choice but to work my hardest to meet them, and as I met them, time and time again, he would increase them until I was far, far ahead of where other children, especially girls, were at my age. I knew nothing different at the time. When I was sent to school, I was leaps and bounds beyond others, causing awe in my classmates and making me both revered and mocked.

The school situation at Miss Prescott's was different in that I was a boarder. I could not escape to home at the end of the school day; there was no reprieve. Being that I was new at the school and not quite in step with the other girls, I craved some space and solitude, and carving this out for myself sidelined me socially even more.

But all wasn't awful. Plus, I discovered a niche for myself in the school plays. I decidedly had a flair for the dramatic and this blossomed in the school theater. I was good at throwing myself into a role, delivering my lines with passion and eloquence. I enjoyed every aspect of it, including the facial makeup we were allowed to apply. I liked it for stage, as well as a means to cover my face, now frequently the host of embarrassing blemishes.

As mentioned, my custom was to create fictional accounts of hurtful situations. This left many wondering what had actually occurred, the lines blurring. What follows is a rendition of what may have happened to a girl I called Marianna.

> Although the performances for the term were over, Marianna continued to apply the makeup, especially the red rouge on her cheeks. Admittedly, she did get heavy-handed with it, which created a bit of a trademark, one that began to annoy. Not seeing the storm brewing around her, it exploded one night at dinner.
>
> In a good mood, which was not common for her at dinnertime, Marianna took her seat and then discovered her classmates with painted cheeks. She froze. When they saw that she noticed their mimicking, they started to laugh, some very hard, and then she saw the teachers and attendants smiling with glee as well. Marianna summoned her strength, forced a smile, and continued with dinner, small-talking with those around her. Once done, she removed herself to her room with no intention of coming out.

> She willed herself into a fit and soon a fever that worried her teachers when they discovered her the next day. This outcome rendered her classmates both sorrowful and repentant.
>
> Marianna recovered and was surrounded by classmates attempting to make it up to her. She seemingly accepted their apologies and company but was plotting revenge. Working her way into their circle and each of their bosoms, they divulged their secrets and she craftily spread them until the whole unit was abuzz and riled.
>
> Soon it became apparent what was happening: there was a traitor within. One evening, as Marianna was heading to her room, a group approached and confronted her about spreading what they had shared in confidence. She stared at them, trying to muster a defense, but none would come, guilt encompassing her entire being.
>
> With no options but to confess or flee, Marianna hurled herself to the ground, forcefully hitting her head on the hearth, rendering herself senseless. Self-injured and defenseless, she was carried to her room and watched over for days as she recovered.
>
> But from this, she never fully recovered, the scar always a reminder of such foolishness. Never again would Marianna plot revenge or wish harm on others, even when she was the target of cruelty and ridicule.

This is a version of my story, similar to the one I included in my travelogue years later. My family and friends wondered if the lead character, Marianna, in this tale was me and how much of the story was true. I never confessed. With my habit of writing some of my most devastating experiences into fictional format, if not all the details applied, it's safe to say that the overall plot and outcome may have.

When I departed the academy at fifteen, I was a stronger, more focused person, one who knew herself better. I always kept in touch with Miss Prescott, who befriended me and comforted me through this storm and others during the year at her school.

Going in, I was aware that Miss Prescott's Academy would not challenge me academically, but I couldn't have known the lessons I would learn and that I would emerge even more driven for distinction.

Maria

I INHERITED BEAUTY. NOT THE EXTRAORDINARY KIND BUT just enough to cause confusion and loss, a magnet attracting me to the shallower things in life. This pull flattered me and in high school offered me a place in the ranks of my peers that then felt sacred.

As a young child, at home and school, I just was. I was me—not a self-conscious me but a me that felt connected to everything, naturally connected, a part of the world I inhabited as well as the people in that world. I didn't feel like more, I didn't feel like less. I felt like I was where I belonged, and it felt so natural that it was nothing.

By fourth grade, I became cognizant that maybe I was less, that maybe there was something wrong or shameful about me. When humiliated, I started to feel embarrassed, and I began to transfer the shame caused by the situation onto myself, that I was wrong, stupid, and deserving of laughter. Some of these now seemingly silly situations fixed their stubborn grip on me and were burned into my memory.

In the fourth grade, the science teacher, Mr. Connelly, chose me to crack an egg in front of the classroom for an experiment. It went badly. He laughed and the entire class laughed as I stood there holding a mess. He derided me about how ridiculous it was that I didn't know how to properly crack an egg. I felt so stupid. I slinked back to my desk feeling hot, ashamed, and confused. Not given an opportunity to say no or to explain that I'd never cracked an egg before, that my mother was too busy with six young children to teach me such a thing left me feeling misunderstood and hurt.

In sixth grade, my teacher asked me to go across the hall and ask for some tissues since we were out of them in our classroom. I knocked on Mr. Locke's door and walked up to him in front of the class. I asked if we could borrow some Kleenex. "Borrow?" he bellowed. "Do you think we want them back when you're done with them?" The class roared with laughter as I stood there feeling like a dope. I held the box of tissues while he continued chuckling, then returned to my classroom, handed the box to Mrs. Boisvert, and took my seat, burning with embarrassment.

Another day in sixth grade as I talked with a couple of boys, a classmate, Lori, approached. Noticeably looking me up and down, she quipped that I looked different. All eyes were on me when, with a grin and a giggle, she announced that it must be because I had washed my hair. As she and the boys laughed, I joined in but felt betrayed. It seemed my dirty secret was more obvious than I realized.

These seemingly harmless situations piled up and began to play with my psyche and put me in my place, a place I'd been shielded from as a young child—the realization that we were what people called "poor." We shared bath water and took shampoos in the sink. We had one bathroom and no shower for a family of eight. The reality that we had a gravel driveway, one beat-up car, one telephone secured to the kitchen wall, no room for more at the kitchen table, and no room in the two bedrooms we shared for sleepovers.

Home still provided the security and comfort we were fortunate to have but could not provide the luxuries and advantages to share and show off to your friends. Home became a refuge and an embarrassing secret at the same time, and it spilled over into how I felt about myself—that somehow, I was not quite enough.

Margaret

ALWAYS ONE FOR WALKS, I DISCOVERED SOLACE IN NATURE, and my health improved being in the fresh air. Walking alone is pleasurable for thinking and clearing the mind but sharing these rambles with others was often preferable to me.

One such adventure started off with a good friend but ended up with me alone. Very alone. This particular ramble became quite well known since I was compelled to share it. I was in Scotland with the Springs, Marcus and Rebecca, with whom I had finally traveled to Europe. We spent over a week in the Highlands, and one day Marcus mentioned climbing the mountain Ben Lomond, which I was immediately in favor of doing.

On the day we planned our hike, we were hoping to get a ride to the mountain but were not able to do so. We headed out on foot, probably leaving later than we should have. We so enjoyed our hike, but as we were heading back, we got turned around. Try as we might, we couldn't find the way out. Seeing I was growing weary, Marcus decided to go ahead and then come back for me or call out for me when he discovered the path. I kept my eyes on him until he disappeared. Then I waited for his return.

The sun was starting to set, and I began to worry. I started to head in the direction he had gone but could not set sights on him. I called his name and heard nothing back. Dusk was falling and I decided I would need to figure this out for myself. I kept walking and walking, calling out to Marcus or anyone who could hear me. But there was no reply and the mist was moving in, cooling the air dramatically.

Soon I was tramping through the mist and darkness, chilled and frightened. It was becoming clear to me that I was going to spend a night alone on this mountain—an unwelcome yet intriguing situation that I could not escape.

At last, I decided I needed to stop walking. I had tripped several times, torn my clothes on unseen branches, and startled myself by stepping into streams and crevices. I found a spot where I could lie down on some brush, plus be out of the elements as much as possible. I was cold and unable to relax, for who knew what roamed this terrain?

I imagined my friends and hosts worrying about me, devising a plan, and sending out search parties. I prayed they would somehow stumble upon me but doubted that would happen at this point in the night. I didn't want to yell out anymore for fear of drawing attention to myself in the dark. I felt vulnerable and wanted to hide more than bring recognition to my plight. I must admit, I did hang my head and sob for a time, the rush of emotion getting the best of me.

Not knowing what time it was or how much time had passed, I resigned myself to hours of waiting. Gazing up to the vast sky with the moon a slice of light, I handed myself over to the universe, taking my mind off my shivering and exhausted body. Although I was not able to relax entirely, I must have fallen into a sort of slumber because soon I could sense the coming of the day. Before I could see any hint of the sunrise, I knew it was breaking. I had heard no loud sounds throughout the night, only the smaller sounds of twigs and leaves, likely birds and squirrels.

When the light began to penetrate, I decided I could manage

well enough to find my way somewhere, hopefully into the path of a person looking for me. It didn't take long for me to be heard and spotted by two shepherds who were part of the makeshift search team. They gasped, letting me know that I probably looked even worse than I felt. I was positively elated that my ordeal was over, and I was going to make it out alive! They insisted on carrying me, which I first resisted but then decided it best.

Back at the lodging, I was welcomed as a miracle—someone coming back from the dead, someone given a second chance at life. People cheered and clapped and hugged me. They wanted to know what I had done to get through the night. Was I hungry? Was I hurt? What did I need? Never had I received such attention! After changing and washing up, I went to lie down, feeling exhausted and feverish. There I stayed for hours as others prepared a celebratory meal to be shared in my honor and for all those who aided in the search.

Some came to my chambers to greet me and to let me know how pleased they were I had survived such an ordeal, knowing that a young boy had recently perished on the mountain after becoming lost. Rebecca, my traveling companion, said that upon hearing the story of the unfortunate boy, she informed the speakers and listeners around her that I was not the sort to allow myself to die up on that mountain. She made it clear I would come out of this very much alive.

Marcus, my companion, survived an almost worse night than I did, feeling terrible that he was unable to make his way back to me and fearing the worst.

Weeks later, after reflecting on this experience, I wrote about it in one of my columns for the *Tribune*. From what I hear, it was quite a topic of conversation among my friends and acquaintances back home. Many were impressed and intrigued by this tale of survival from such a defenseless creature as me! But I was reminded of my resilience and my propensity to dig deep in challenging situations. Oh, what we learn about ourselves when forced to function in survival mode. I hoped I would not have to test myself in quite this way again.

Maria

I DIDN'T BEGIN TO GET SCARED UNTIL WE RAN INTO another group of lost hikers, and one of the women in that group had injured her leg and was being carried by others. Suddenly, the situation seemed much more dangerous than I had realized.

It was a classic fall day, and our departure to the mountain was a little too late, it seems. There were about eight of us girls, several a few years older than me, who decided to climb Mount Monadnock, an ideal hiking mountain near our hometown. My three sisters were part of this group.

We arrived at the base and started our ascent. I, being my scrawny, wild self at the time, was a bundle of energy and easily ran circles around some of the others. I wore my favorite Wacky Pack tee-shirt that read Captain Crutch with an image of Captain Crunch waving a crutch in the air. I also wore my suede desert boots, one of which had lost its stitching at the toe. I was as carefree as my head of unkempt curls, as was the rest of our climbing crew.

We scrambled up the mountain, traversing trickling streams and jumping from rock to rock. We stopped at all the views along the way, captivated by the miles and miles we could see from our perches. After finally arriving at the top, we played for a long time, sliding down long, flat rocks and in hysterics when my sister stood up at the bottom after one run with the butt of her blue jeans completely gone. She hurriedly tied her jacket around her waist to cover the embarrassing reveal. Not long after that, while scrambling up a rock, I caught the loose flap of my desert boot and ripped almost the entire sole off. Because it was impossible to walk with it flapping so much, to the laughter of my companions, I tore off the entire bottom and kept the suede shoe top around my ankle.

After our shenanigans at the summit, we headed back down, but darkness had started to move in, and soon we could not see the markings on the trees and rocks that led us along the path. We did not have flashlights. We had run out of snacks and water. And before long, we were lost. We had no clue where the correct path was and became more and more turned around. We decided to use the buddy system, each of us taking the hand of another and sticking close together, no couple leaving the pack.

We roamed and roamed, the crackling of twigs under our feet growing louder and louder in the quiet forest night. I remember holding my little sister's hand and relying heavily on the older ones to lead the way, to find our way to safety. Occasionally, someone would yell out, "Help!" hoping someone would hear us. All we knew was that we were indeed going downhill, so that was good, but each step in the darkness was an unknown since we couldn't see anything at all.

For all our playful spirit earlier, we were now filled with regret that we had not prepared properly, that we had not started our venture early enough, that we were foolish and as such, were paying a price. Suddenly, Captain Crutch wasn't so funny and the piece of suede swaying around my ankle was doing nothing to protect my poor right foot.

Miraculously, one time when we yelled for help, we received a response. We all cheered! "We're over here!" we chimed. Another group of hikers made their way to us, supporting the hiker who had fallen and hurt her leg.

After what seemed like hours more of attempting to make our way down the mountain, we did indeed arrive in a clearing and could see a light in the distance, which turned out to be a lodge. From there we were able to locate our parents, who had arrived at the mountain earlier, worried about us, and had dispatched a search team. We were so relieved to have made it down and to not have to wander the mountain all night long, terrified and cold. Our parents were relieved too and didn't lecture us too badly, knowing we had already recognized the errors of our ways.

Years later, we still laughed about the antics of that day, and how we lost ourselves in the utter joy of the moment at the top.

Margaret

Growing up in Cambridge and Boston, I was never far from water, never far from the ocean. Being one always drawn to the therapeutic and awe-inspiring qualities of nature, the ocean offered me much. Again, me being me and endearing myself to others so readily, I was invited most summers to spend months at the ocean, often with friends in Rhode Island.

As with all of nature, I was entranced by the mystery as well as the terror of the sea. But unlike the rest of nature, the ocean could truly frighten me. It whispered things to me I did not want to hear, filling me with dread at times, but I would shake the feeling and embrace it once again.

I relished meandering beach walks and lying in bed at night, the window open, listening to the waves move in on the shore. One particular night, my hosts and I ventured out to view the full moon above the restless black body of the night ocean. Their house was quite directly onshore, and being high tide, there was not much of a beach, but there were large rocks to sit and lean on. Cloaked in the moonlight, we admired this exceptional night, when out of what seemed nowhere a massive and powerful wave moved in on us, sending us scrambling across the rocks for what seemed our lives. That moment, caught off guard, we were reminded that the most spectacular display of nature often combines an element of life-threatening surprise. This was not the last time I would experience such a juxtaposition.

For years after, when we laid eyes on land, when the shores of New York were in sight, when I believed we would make it home and step foot safely on shore, I was taken by terrifying surprise and sensed that this time there would be no way to scramble to safety.

Maria

THE COUPLE OF DAYS A YEAR THAT WE MADE IT OVER TO the coast for time at the beach were some of the best. Fitting eight people into a station wagon full of supplies was a feat, so usually our vacations were closer by, the coast being a solid two-hour drive from where we lived. Yet most summers my parents would manage to get us to the beach, partly, I believe, because my mother loved it so much herself that a summer without at least one visit to the coast would not be right.

With our tattered towels, gigantic cardboard tub of potato chips, peanut butter sandwiches, and a jug of Kool-Aid, we settled onto the sand for a full day at the beach. The melody of the waves, the lure of the sand—oh, for us children, excitement was at its highest. We'd stay in the ocean as long as we could, holding hands and skipping over the waves, and as we got older, diving beneath them and swimming around. We never did learn how to properly wrangle the ocean. Neither of our parents were familiar enough with it to give real sound advice, but we figured a few things out. Enough to survive a day or two.

One of my favorite ways to mingle with the ocean, especially when I was young, was to sit in the shallows with my siblings and let the waves roll us around as though we were shells tossed onto shore. Occasionally, a wave would be much more than expected, taking us by surprise and truly tumbling us around like rag dolls. That scared me and taught me to respect one of the strongest shows of Mother Nature that exists.

As we got older, it was harder to fit us all in one car to make the trip, and we began to travel to the coast with friends who had cars. Those trips for me were never as thrilling as the ones as a child because I would hardly notice the water, let alone hang out in it for hours. The focus in high school was the friends I was with, especially the boys I hoped to impress or the tan I was attempting to acquire that day so that when we went out that night, I would sport that special glow that only the sun can bestow.

Margaret

WITH A CORE BELIEF THAT OUR PURPOSE IN LIFE IS TO GROW, I found it impossible to turn down an invitation that would yield a firsthand view and understanding of our country's rapid expansion. When friends invited me on a trip to the burgeoning Midwest, I immediately set out to find a way to make this happen.

After my father's passing, I became the organizer of the household, from finances to our daily functioning to the education of my younger siblings. My mother, always more reserved, and due to years of worry and loss, a fragile sort of woman, depended upon me. I, being the oldest and especially a daughter, could not but step up to this role. I had passed up other offers of travel to uphold my responsibilities, but this one beckoned powerfully.

After much consideration and discussion, yes, I would venture west with my companions, and all at home were supportive and willing to make do without me for the majority of the summer of 1843. I could feel the excitement of this journey in my heart and mind, to discover life outside of New England, which was quite settled and predictable. I longed to see how those packing up and moving westward, settling new towns and cities, making a life on the prairies and along the Great Lakes, were living. How much I was looking forward to a firsthand account of such a new frontier.

Packing for the trip, I was aware of how I was leaving many of the conveniences of home behind. That was a little daunting but again, more thrilling because I was that kind of person and traveler. I gave myself over to where I was, drinking thirstily from the fountains of new environs with fresh ideas and perspectives. How better to gain clarity on the direction of our country and the changing lives of our citizens than to meld into their style of living for days and weeks?

We would be spending some nights at establishments and

others with host families, families who would open their homes to us, feed us, entertain us. There were a couple of stops where my companions were unable to secure accommodations in advance, but we would find a place to spend the night once we arrived and could see and talk with those there. I believed there was always a solution, especially where other people were involved.

The energy was high as the group set out by coach, our first stop—Niagara Falls. Having always been drawn to the ocean—to the rhythm, the predictable sound of waves crashing on the shore and onto the rocky coast—I expected a similar affinity to the sound of the Falls.

To an extent, I was soothed and entranced by the Falls but after a rather short time, the roar of the Falls, without an ebb and flow, started to overwhelm and swallow me. I found, due to the massive sound, I could best enjoy the Falls for moments at a time. When the vision and sound were in unison, the whole experience captivated me in a wondrous way. Moments in though, I was saturated with their beauty, the merciless power would begin to overtake my senses, and I would need to recede. How very different from the ocean with its breath licking the shores was the Falls' unending pounding of water to earth.

I could see how the Falls captivated and spawned a multitude of dwellings around them. As we moved on, it was not only the scenery that offered beauty and newness but the lifestyle of those living there.

Maria

IT WAS A SNEAK PEEK, A GLIMPSE INTO THE SATISFACTION OF losing oneself in the search. I was a senior in high school and writing a paper on a topic that genuinely interested me. I was researching fact versus fiction in Leon Uris's QB VII. One day, after school, I mustered the courage to enter the local college library and once there, dived into finding sources. Poring over these, I mined for information that would support my position.

I was there for hours, lost to time. I had not experienced such abandon since, I imagined, my childhood. When I finally snapped out of it and looked at the clock, I was shocked to see it was dinnertime already, after which I needed to get to confirmation rehearsal. I raced home, ate quickly, and hurried to the church. Sitting in the pew as the priest informed us about what we were signing on to, I was still on a high from my experience at the library and couldn't wait to get back to my paper. It was the first time I had felt this way about an assignment. I was excited to immerse myself in the learning and felt like, in the end, I would have something valuable to share.

The priest then asked what saint's name we had chosen for our confirmation name, and I realized I hadn't even considered this. When the person taking down the names came to me, I looked into her face, pleading for suggestions. She said I could take my name, Maria, meaning Mary. That would be fine, she nodded. I agreed. How silly—to take my own name as my confirmation name—I thought later.

When rehearsal was over, my classmate Henry offered me a ride home on his bicycle. Feeling good, and even though I had a skirt on, I sat on the handlebars, and he rode me home, my hair waving in the cool night air. It was a day I'd always remember—the day I discovered the thrill of the quest for knowledge, the quest for truth. The off-white cowl neck and pale beige skirt I was wearing that day added to this revelatory feeling and the lightness that accompanied it.

Margaret

On my visit to the Midwest, two issues pressed on me exceedingly, the first being the infringement on the territory of the Indians. I was immediately captivated by their way of life, the way they spent their days and time, the beauty of their people, and the ingenious way they interacted with the natural setting around them. Although persecuted and treated unjustly, there remained an elegance, an integrity, a distinct spirit that pervaded who they were and all they did.

How horrible I felt that we had claimed their land, invaded their space and in their attempt to defend themselves, painted them to seem as heathens and savages when those were masks we often touted. How tragic that we had pushed them to the fringes and tried to recreate them in our likeness, when so much of who they were and how they lived was, in ways, superior to our own. Whenever I could, I would sit with the Indian women and children, welcomed to partake in the preparation of meals, rituals, and daily tasks of these industrious, generous people. My heart hurt for them. My heart hurt for all of us.

From other Americans, I heard tales of heroic Indians and their chiefs, those with almost superpowers; I also heard horrendous stories of savagery, these usually provoked by the insensitive encroachment of the whites.

What sickened and concerned me was the evident motive of many who were pushing west: the one-sided desire for monetary gain regardless of how this impacted the natural beauty and balance of the land and the peoples already there. This was hard to observe and reinforced a concern I had held for a while—the focus on materialism as the single goal and gain of any venture, especially as the ultimate aim of our country.

Oh, how I also felt for so many of the women who had set out with their husbands and families to set up a new life in the wilderness of these prairies and lands around these enormous lakes, rarely by their choice. How ill-equipped they were to deal with this new lifestyle, being used to the more civilized and convenient households of the long-settled towns of New England. It was almost torturous, managing households without the domestic help they were used to, raising children in isolation from extended family and established churches and schools, collecting firewood and preparing meals from what they had in their possession as there was often no local market to purchase what they desired or needed.

I found many of these women depressed, overwhelmed, and regretful of the life they'd left behind where more luxury and leisure were theirs. Whereas the men communed with one another and busied themselves with working the land and hunting—a radical new way of life—the women were left to do what they had been doing back home but without any of the support and comforts they had known, creating a distinct sense of loss and sorrow.

Yet, not to paint the picture as all bleak, how satisfactorily so much of the progress was going and how admirably so many of the families fared. Many were able to construct the kind of life they wanted here. They were able to transplant the best of what they had back home, yet added to it the treasures of this new land. Many were able to acquire musical instruments and to entertain one another in the evening with the most precious music. The children of many families appeared well adjusted, with an intelligence and brightness that gave hope for the future. These new houses were spacious and, although not as refined as those in New England, possessed their own awesome space and character.

One night, with no prearranged lodging and no family to open their doors to us, we ended up spending the night in a barroom. I never imagined myself in such an accommodation, but when one is tired enough, even a pool table will do. Once the owner had cleared the room for us women to slumber, we all found some sort of surface to pillow our heads and sleep. Fortunately, this was not the norm of our trip, but it certainly made for a night we would not readily forget!

There were many days when I set off on my own to explore and marvel at the sights. Other times, I was escorted around on the lake by Indians in their boats and led on horseback by locals who had come to know the territory well and were anxious to share the beauty with those who would take it back and tell others about the great life they had made for themselves out west. They wanted to assure others that they were not fools for leaving all they had left behind for this new life.

Most still believed that this risk offered them more than they could ever hope for in New England, and for many, it was true.

Maria

My first name wasn't common where I grew up in New Hampshire, so I was usually the only Maria in any given setting, school or work. I was often reminded that it was Italian for Mary, and indeed that's what my Italian grandfather called me and that felt special, growing up Catholic. And it's a musical name, one that would regularly trigger songs—"I've just met a girl named Maria," or "How do you solve a problem like Maria?" and even "Ave Maria." My sister Laura later informed me it was one of the most common woman's names in the world, and I have come to understand that.

I was vocal about not wanting to be called Marie, which sometimes people defaulted to as a nickname for Maria. I didn't have a problem with the name Marie, it just wasn't mine. Only my father could call me Marie, which occasionally he did, with tenderness.

Honestly, I was embarrassed by my middle name. Frances didn't sit well with me. It seemed like a name for an old man, which is where my parents got it from—two older male family members. I dreaded when anyone asked me what my middle name was and resorted to lying about it for years, telling people it was Francine since that happened to be the name of one of Barbie Doll's blond friends at the time. I knew names mattered—they were the first handle on poking fun at someone or deriving an impression of them before even meeting them.

My initials, MFD, which I noticed on the toothpaste box was the abbreviation for "manufactured," had a good ring to them when I played radio station, sitting for hours on a hassock in front of the hi-fi stereo: *This is MFD radio station wishing you a good day and playing some of your favorites to get you through.* Whoever said I could never be on the radio because of my lisp was not aware that I had my own station for years in the comfort of my dining room, and no one criticized me. Then again, was anyone tuning in?

Margaret

It probably seemed odd that I decided to go with my middle name, Margaret, since my mother's name was Margarett. I got some kickback from family members, but overall it was understood that when I made a decision, that was it. I'm sure it baffled and hurt my parents since they had given me the name Sarah, and in their minds, I would always be their Sarah Margaret, but they too came to accept me as Margaret, a better fit. I knew Margaret, from the Greek, means pearl, luminous gem, and that resonated with me more than Sarah, which means princess.

When I claimed authorship to a piece, I took various approaches. *Summer on the Lakes*, in 1843, I signed S. M. Fuller, but *Women in the Nineteenth Century*, I signed S. Margaret Fuller. I marked my columns in the *Tribune* with an asterisk. Many knew it was me, but I wanted to mask gender from my pieces since I didn't want them dismissed or misjudged because of my being a woman. The asterisk made my columns appear more neutral and perhaps a bit more intriguing, signed with a star.

I finished writing *Summer on the Lakes* on my birthday. I completed *Woman in the Nineteenth Century* on my birthday as well. Did I plan it this way? Perhaps, but anyone who writes knows that a work isn't truly finished until it proclaims itself to be.

My sister Ellen and her husband, Ellery, named their first child after me. If I had had a daughter, I would have named her Julia Adelaide. I would have resurrected that beautiful girl laid out perfectly in death for me to see as a three-year-old. I would have brought her back to life as my daughter.

Many would criticize that such an intellectual as myself would attribute significance to such things as names, dates, objects, dreams, or chance interactions. But I asked, was the human mind and spirit not big enough to hold it all? All the marvels and wonders, sciences and philosophies of the world and beyond? As with the sexes, why not embrace all within us, the feminine and the masculine? Why must we constantly set limits on ourselves?

THREE

Maria

I WAS SLOWLY MAKING AN ASCENT TO LIKING LIFE. I WAS IN graduate school in New Hampshire when a friend from northern Ireland I had met on the kibbutz informed me he was in New York City. Two of my sisters and my brother-in-law, who was working as a restaurant manager for the Grand Hyatt, lived there. We all ended up together for a leisurely brunch at the hotel.

The physical details long hazy, what remained was the strong feeling of complete contentment; how suddenly, there descended upon me a feeling of utter happiness and satisfaction I hadn't recalled feeling before. I imagined it came from above, and it flowed over me with such ferocity that I stopped and looked up. I thought, if I were to die tomorrow, it would be OK because at this very moment, I am good. I felt fulfilled and as though I had been released, my struggle within momentarily melting. I wished I could have experienced this feeling longer or called upon it at will but that its impression stayed with me seemed the most I could ask for.

A few years later, there was another. During such a routine task as brushing my teeth, I was forced to do a double take in the mirror. Something had flashed, compelling me to stop and look deep into my eyes as though they were another person's. Locking my own gaze, I was seized by a strange knowing, a knowing that I mattered, that I was destined to do something. I often revisited that image of me at that moment and questioned its validity. Me? Really? I'd become convinced that every life has great value, so, yes, I supposed it was true. But on my bolder days, when I believed in myself, I knew it to be certain.

It occurred to me that my destiny might resemble an echo. We've all heard echoes, the reflection of sound not unlike the reflection in a mirror. To cast something forward, even something previously articulated, a reverberation that contributes to the continued evolution of our minds and hearts—that is indeed something, an echo.

Margaret

When you experience a groundbreaking moment with yourself, it's sacred and you never forget. I was a rather young girl when I experienced my first encounter with knowing that I was connected to something bigger than myself.

It was an overcast day, and Father was in Washington, D.C., as usual. Mother and I were in the parlor working on our letter to Father to let him know what was going on in the household and to report on my progress with the lessons he had left for me. Mother had a baby on her lap and another playing around the room.

I remember the moment so well, but the surrounding details have faded, so what I have described as the setting in the household will have to do. For some reason, I was bounding up the stairs. Either we had finished our task and I was set free, or I was on my way to fetch something. Suddenly, I was stopped in my tracks. There was a window there, but I didn't look out the window. I wasn't looking at anything outside of myself. I was gazing up and looking down at myself at the same time, compelled to ask: Who am I and what am I meant for? These questions gripped me solidly, and although the answers did not reveal themselves entirely, a great clarity descended on me, a massive response that indicated to me at that moment, on that spot, that I was someone significant, that I was to leave a mark on the world. Once the spell was broken and I continued my way upstairs, I knew. I was aware from that point on that there was great meaning for me on Earth and that I was destined to do important work.

Years later, on Thanksgiving Day, I experienced another revelation. No longer a young girl, now twenty-one, we had moved from Cambridge to the farm in Groton, Massachusetts. Father was no longer in politics and desired a different, what he considered healthier, lifestyle. I was angered and depressed about our move. Leaving all my friends and connections behind was devastating. I was determined to get back to Cambridge and Boston as often as possible, but now that I was away, my life became more consumed by helping with domestics and tutoring other children as well as my siblings. I was struggling terribly with this relocation from a personal standpoint.

It was a cold and gray New England Thanksgiving Day, and we had gone to church. It was a long, tedious ceremony, and looking around at the people there, I became increasingly irritated and frustrated to be stuck with townsfolk who appeared too ordinary and simple for the work and goals I had for myself. With this angst building inside of me, I fled the church immediately when the service ended. I ran toward the woods by the church, tears burning down my cheeks. Lift me from here! Save me, I begged.

After running a distance, then walking as fast as my legs would move, I threw myself down onto a bed of leaves by a small stream and lay there quietly sobbing. After a few moments, I looked up at the natural world around me and was struck by the distinct realization that I was a part of this landscape; that my being there was as natural as the quiet babbling of the stream, the cushion of leaves beneath me, and the trees forming a canopy over my being. I was one in this moment with this place, and I was one with this world.

I looked up amid revelation as the sun began to fight its way through the thick, gray clouds just enough to cast a ray through the woods. Just enough for me to see that it was going to be all right. Just enough for me to decide to embrace my life and duties as they revealed themselves now. Fighting where I was in this moment, viewing it as miserable and unfair, and feeling sorry for myself were not going to set me free. Letting go of my sense of self and faithfully fulfilling my duties with love and generosity would somehow be my ticket.

Maria

THERE ARE SO MANY WAYS TO GET LOST, BUT THE WORST was losing myself, how it happened without realizing, and how I ended up roaming the darkness of every day.

When I was teaching high school English, we read a book titled *Walkabout*. It has an involved plot but what fascinated most was the idea of this young aboriginal boy released in the vast wilderness of Australia, forced to survive, to rely on himself completely, and to find his way home. His tribe prepared and blessed him and awaited his return. He would return transformed by surviving the harsh terrain and coming in the closest contact with himself possible. When and if he returned, he'd be celebrated. He would have survived the most intense of initiations, a very clear and deliberate rite of passage.

My students and I read this book with awe and detachment. It seemed like another era or another planet even, but inside I longed for such an experience, one with all the ingredients that accompanied such an initiation. I longed for that deliverance.

In class, we discussed rites of passage and the initiations we'd experienced or would experience. Somehow, for good or bad, they didn't measure up to the likes of a walkabout.

A couple of the students were Eagle Scouts, which seemed the closest we might come to a walkabout experience. I confessed I had been a Brownie, then a Girl Scout, even a Cadet for a while. I earned my badges and participated in flying-up ceremonies. As Girl Scouts, we had annual weekend campouts, ahead of which we'd weave sit-upons from newspapers, covering them snuggly in plastic. We put up tents and dug latrines. We hiked with sticks, cooked eggs in orange peels, and told ghost stories around the campfire. By Sunday, I couldn't wait for my parents to pick me up.

Religious rites came up as well. Growing up Catholic, I made my first communion and was confirmed. For some reason, the year I made my first holy communion, the priests decided to have us sit with our families, not sit together at the front of the church; there was no ceremony at all, really. It also did not take place in the traditional month of May either, rather, around Thanksgiving, and I distinctly recall wearing my faux fur coat over my dress. But my veil was visible, and after the priest mentioned there were some of us in the congregation making our first communion that day, several people noticed me and offered me Kennedy half-dollars and dollar bills.

My communion photograph was of me alone, standing in front of the fireplace, the swoop in my hair mimicking the Thanksgiving cornucopia hanging on the wall above, not the usual large group of children standing on the cement steps of the church, hands folded, dressed in white, squinting in the May sunshine.

In class, the students shouted out other rites of passage and what they signified—graduating, getting a driver's license, being able to vote at eighteen, and legally drinking at whatever age it happened to be then. It was a mixed bag at best.

I had to wonder whether I, the girl who ran for her life after putting the trash out at the curb after dark, would survive a walkabout. Would I ever make it back?

Margaret

It was a magnificent invitation and one I was more ready for than I realized. In ways, I felt I had outgrown some of my friends in New England. Many remained in their heads, continuing the search within, while I was feeling the pull to look outside of myself as well, to strike a balance. I wanted more of a chance to witness current issues firsthand, to spotlight the inequities, to instigate momentum for change. The move to a new city to examine these issues was enticing, especially a move to New York.

Relief from the constant quest for money was also appealing. I had completed two teaching stints, both exhausting and doing little to mitigate my financial straits, especially the one that never paid! My role as the first editor of *The Dial* was an enormous amount of work for which I was not compensated either.

My most fruitful endeavor was the Conversations series I held for women in Boston. They were well attended and successful in many ways, including monetarily. All of these experiences were enriching and offered me much beyond their financial outcome, but with my obligations, mine was an unenviable situation overall.

When offered a position with a paper that would compensate me well and move me to a location where I could further my mission for social reform, I eagerly said yes. Many of my friends did not want me to accept Horace Greeley's offer with the *New York Tribune*, some because they didn't necessarily grasp what was best for me and others because New York City seemed unrefined compared to Boston and other parts of New England. Perhaps not a safe place for a single woman.

I had been held back for so many years being the dutiful daughter and sister. I ached to step out of my confines and into something more exciting and rewarding. One factor that made the move less daunting to others was that I would live with the Greeleys initially, so it wasn't as though I was setting up on my own to start.

I adored the Greeleys' sprawling house on the banks of the East River. The best of both worlds, it offered an appealing natural setting with views of ships gliding up and down the glassy river, yet was a doable commute to the bustling heart of the city and the *Tribune* office. I struggled with deadlines, especially now that I was writing for a daily paper, but I kept my head above water. Mr. Greeley did express some frustration at times, but I delivered good columns, so he was appeased by this.

In addition to my literary columns, I started to write more social commentary about the living conditions of immigrants, the imprisonment of women, and the treatment of the mentally inferior. Writing about such topics required me to visit these places, which was both riveting and appalling. My brother Lloyd, with his own partial inferiority, afforded me a genuine interest in the treatment of his kind, and I visited both the Bloomingdale and Blackwell asylums.

I also spent time with female prisoners at Sing Sing, and although our life experiences did not have all that much in common, I came from the place that as sisters, we needed to understand and support one another. I prayed my presence and words offered some comfort and hope and that my columns about the compromised position of women in our society, in addition to my book, assisted in creating continued momentum toward more equal and fair treatment. I believed in the opportunity for women to be rehabilitated, to be granted another chance, and to be supported in this second chance through programming, although truth be known, most of these women never had even one chance. Not one.

Just before my move to New York City, I expanded an article I originally wrote for *The Dial* into book form. It was to become a bestseller in the United States and abroad. *Woman in the Nineteenth Century* was my earnest plea for a true examination of the unfair and damaging treatment of women—treatment that was a major disservice to all women and that I felt should be brought to light. With two books under my belt and my notable skill as an intellectual and conversationalist, I was well-positioned to press forward on behalf of truth and justice.

I became comfortable in this new city and made connections rather quickly. Soon I was able to secure my own place, which allowed the Greeleys their space back to deal with their issues without me there to buffer what perhaps needed to be aired. Most weeks I spent an evening or more with other writers and artists in the city. I was busy and highly motivated by the constant stimulation of this rapidly growing city—one that offered enormous abundance.

Maria

While an undergraduate, I spent two summers in New York City with my oldest sister, Ceil. It was gracious of her to invite me, but that was what she did, being the oldest, often feeling responsible for our well-being. She could see I was floundering without a clear direction and feeling down about myself and rather dismal in general. It was also helpful that I would be subletting and assisting with the rent over the summer. I suppose it was a win-win. I knew she didn't have to ask me but she did. Because, again, I was no prize then, and her invitation reflected the size of her heart.

My first summer there we lived in Greenwich Village, on Bedford Street in a quaint brownstone. We loved the location, not far from Washington Square. I quickly discovered the place was quite infested with cockroaches, which was not uncommon, but being new to me, these little creatures made an impression. When the lights went down, they came out, just doing their thing, not bothering us. But knowing they were marching around kept me, a light sleeper anyway, often with one eye open.

The only air conditioner was in the bedroom where we ended up spending a lot of our time. Without much light and always cool, it became "the cave." My first morning in the city, with Ceil already at work, I found stepping out of the building and onto the street dizzying. I turned in circles a couple of times before I oriented myself in the direction I believed I needed to go.

I had registered for a course at the School of Visual Arts, thinking I might want a career in commercial arts. But I only lasted a few weeks with that possibility. My interest fizzled with the first assignment where I had to design a milk carton. My sketch didn't come out as I envisioned and in no way measured up to the others in my class or with what I believed were my instructor's expectations. I hastily quit, and what I felt most bad about was that my sister's boyfriend had paid for the course. Neither he nor my sister made me feel bad, which was a relief. I did need to find summer work, so when the idea of contacting a temp agency came up, I followed the lead. Since I would only be there for a couple of months, it sounded like the most reasonable approach to employment.

I ended up in two temp jobs that summer, the longest-running one in Battery Park at an investment firm called AG Becker where I was a receptionist in the human resources office. I answered phones, transferred calls, and took down messages. The head of human resources was Mr. Tulley, a Lou Grant look-alike. He'd strut around the office of primarily women, stopping to chat here and there and grabbing a coffee at the beverage cart. When he'd look my way, I'd muster a feeble hello but didn't receive anything back but a blank stare. I'm sure he knew I was a temp filling in for one of his staff who was on vacation. I understood I was basically a nonentity, and I liked it that way.

Occasionally, something would be delivered for Mr. Tulley, and I'd have to bring it to his office. If the door was open, I could do a little knock on the doorjamb, tiptoe in, leave the package or envelope, and exit silently. Often, he was on the phone and would glance my way, and I'd nod and exit. One day I delivered a package and he wasn't on the phone and wasn't absorbed in the paperwork on his desk. He was looking directly at me as I entered with an oversized envelope in my hands. Then he spoke. I stopped dead in my tracks, startled.

"You know, if you lost some weight," he said, "you'd be a real good-looking girl."

I set the envelope on his desk, uttered a garbled thank you, and raced back to my desk with my head down. Mr. Tulley spoke to me. Mr. Tulley noticed that I'm fat. Mr. Tulley thinks I could be pretty. Mr. Tulley both shot me down and lifted me up with one comment.

My head was spinning. I didn't know whether I should laugh or cry. Or maybe I should be angry? He's one to talk, that fat, bald, ugly man who feels he can make judgments about young women. He can and he did. That comment carried as much clout as Mr. Tulley knew it would.

So that summer I continued to dream about being skinny. I fantasized about me in my Levi's jeans with a navy blue turtleneck tucked in over my flat abdomen and bony hips, the ideal image of thinness that my sister and I always agreed upon.

Early in the morning I would get up, pull on shorts, a tee, and my sneakers, grab my Walkman with the Olivia Newton-John cassette "Let's Get Physical" in it, and head to Washington Square where I would jog around and around in the company of many. I would get lost in the herd of runners and in the music. "Let me hear your body talk, body talk . . . " But if my body was talking, I wasn't listening. I disliked it, and I had little desire to get physical since I wasn't comfortable in my own skin. But I had that ideal in my head, and when I achieved that, I knew all would be good. Until then, I'd try to lie low and discipline myself until I reached my goal.

Part of this scheme was that I wouldn't allow myself to have fun because I wasn't and couldn't be happy. Yet. I'd sit in a low beach chair in the middle of the living room watching TV at night, sipping a diet cream soda. No, the couch was too comfortable and yes, the diet soda was enough. It tasted good and had no calories. Instead of expanding my horizons in NYC, I was shrinking my world to what I felt I could control, to what I felt I deserved. I was obsessed. Obsessed with the fact that I didn't measure up and the evidence of this was that I was overweight. Even Mr. Tulley noticed.

Margaret

RESIDING WITH THE GREELEYS WHEN I WAS FIRST WRITING for the *Tribune* was a delight. I loved the ramshackle house at Turtle Bay, especially the wildly overgrown grounds. This scenic setting was especially enjoyable when my new friend, Nathan James, and his dog visited me there. We passed many pleasant hours on the banks of that river.

I was fortunate throughout my life that employers, friends, and sometimes total strangers were generous in offering me shelter, places to both live for a while or simply visit. Maybe it had to do with my being a single woman, labeled by some an old maid in need of aid, or maybe it had more to do with my magnetism and notoriety. Be what may, I appreciated the Greeleys opening their home to me, and oh, how much you learn about others when you share living space.

The Greeleys were very strict with their food and drink. They even stayed away from tea, worrying that such a beverage would in some way impact their health negatively. They were careful not to say much to me about my habits. I was fond, or shall I say very fond, of my strong cups of coffee. It was mentioned now and then by Mr. Greeley that such a habit as this, the drinking of strong coffee, might be contributing to my periodic ill health, especially my headaches. But I did not consider changing such a thing as my coffee consumption or any other habit of mine. I was feeling strong and productive and thriving in this new environment. Plus, I could see no advantages that their strict dietary habits afforded them that made me want to follow their lead. So I tolerated the almost daily disapproving glances from my hosts, smiling secretly to myself as I stirred my potion with a silver spoon.

I had grown very fond of their little son, Arthur, called Pickie, as I had of Waldo's little boy. We had a close and lovely connection, the two of us spending hours together on the porch as I read and he dallied around. Perhaps I attached so readily to sweet little children and them to me because of the one I had lost in my arms. Perhaps these little ones offered me another chance to bestow my unconditional love, my hopes and dreams onto them. I had emotionally overwhelming moments when I longed deeply for a child of my own and wondered if I would ever have an opportunity to be a loving mother, not a loving sister and friend only. It seemed more and more unlikely that being a mother was in store for me.

Maria

My second summer in New York City had a pulse. I knew my way around and what to expect. Stepping out onto the street my first morning there was not as daunting as it had been the year before. Plus, my sister had moved to the Upper East Side, which was easier to navigate than the Village. I agreed to a waitressing position at the restaurant where she was working. They needed new hires to cover for those who had left the city for the summer, so I was spared job hunting. Rascals appeared to be a fun place with a rustic interior and sawdust and peanut shells on the floor. I had a fair amount of table-waiting experience too, so I approached the job with a dash of confidence.

Unlike my previous summer, instead of a stiff, sterile office environment, I was racing around on sawdust in sneakers and an apron. I was surrounded by these hip New Yorkers, feeling a bit uncool and country bumpkin-like, but there were worse things for sure, and I liked the pace and intensity. My cut of the tips at the end of each shift was substantial, and since I was putting myself through college, it was necessary to bank as much money as possible. Although I worked at school too, it helped to know that along with financial aid, I may have enough funds to make it through the fall semester.

Every January, my father lined up the federal financial aid forms on the dining room table—four or five of them, depending on the year—and systematically filled them all out. I appreciated that he did that for us, but that was about all he could do, so it was up to each one of us to earn what other funds we needed. The healthy tips at the restaurant filled that need.

Although not fully embraced as a true Rascal's staff member, being a summer fill-in, I did OK, especially since they all knew I was Ceil's younger sister. It was pretty dog-eat-dog, so that connection provided some protection. Some returning customers would ask for the girl from New Hampshire. They thought I was genuinely sweet—a rarity in that environment—and I blushed at being singled out in this corny way.

The practice of pooling tips created an atmosphere of eliminating the lowest common denominator. If a waiter was not pulling their weight and therefore yielding lower tips, they would be reported to management and gone within days. The moral of the story was to earn your keep because it was attached to everyone else's. No room for incompetence or slackers at Rascal's.

My comfort with the city and small gains in self-confidence lured me from the apartment more often that summer. I visited museums on my own and Central Park quite often, roller-skating on Sunday mornings when a big section of the park was closed to traffic. A couple of friends invited me to concerts, and I said yes to these invitations, the mayhem and music at these events enticing me to loosen my grip. It was a relief to lighten up on the self-punitive approach I had clung to the previous summer.

Margaret

It wasn't necessary for me to go into the *Tribune* office every day. Some days I could work from the Greeleys' on the Upper East Side. The window of my room overlooked the river, and working at my desk, I had an inspiring view. When my task was to read books for review, it didn't seem worth the lengthy commute into the city. Instead, I could swing and read on the front porch with Pickie occupying himself at my feet.

But most days, I needed to make the trek. There was a bit of a hike from the house to the street where I would catch the Harlem omnibus to the *Tribune* building downtown. I enjoyed walking the grassy path from the house to the street if it wasn't too muddy, snowy, or bitterly cold. The ride into the city could be a tedious one, the bus crowded and making frequent stops, but I was usually up to the commute, my head filled with ideas and thoughts about the articles I would produce that day. This position required regular and strict deadlines, and although Mr. Greeley was quite patient with me and others, there was only room for so much understanding when you had a paper to send to press every single day. Not all survived in this harried environment, including my brother-in-law Ellery Channing. Although I recommended him for the job, his not having what it took reinforced that he should be where he belonged—home with his wife, my sister Ellen.

For some reason, Ellery could never settle, never fully apply himself, leaving my sister to wonder why she married him and even more puzzling, why he married her. Me, I learned the hard way to watch out for ones like Ellery—ones who searched for what others could do for them. After his performance at the *Tribune*, I didn't recommend him to anyone I knew even if it might have benefited my sister somehow; soon I was convinced it never would.

I'd finally arrive at the building and climb the stairs from the printing press operations to an open room above furnished with long tables at which the journalists would sit to scribble out their columns and news stories. I had my own space, which I appreciated. It was stacked with books I was to review for my columns. When not reviewing books, art, and music, I visited institutions so I could call for reform, knowing firsthand the current conditions.

As the only woman writing for the *Tribune* then, my presence was regarded as an oddity, but by that time I was used to being an outsider, someone who was good at what she did yet still was not accepted.

One of my fellow journalists and literary critics at the time, writing for the *Broadway Journal*, was Edgar Allan Poe. We didn't spend much time together outside of literary gatherings we both attended, but I admired and respected his work and he expressed the same for me, praising my *Woman in the Nineteenth Century* highly. Aside from this, we lived different lifestyles and did lose patience with one another on occasion.

Perhaps I did become overly involved. While Mr. Poe carried on what appeared to be an affair with a married woman, a second woman, feeling scorned by him, decided to make this thinly veiled situation public. Desperate, the first woman pleaded with me to assist her in collecting her items, specifically her letters, from Mr. Poe. She had repeatedly asked him to deliver them back to her, and he had not fulfilled her request.

Normally, I would not agree to such a task for the primary reason that I was always busy and tried to avoid such pettiness, but I had become incensed by men holding women hostage in ruinous situations for their own gain. Mr. Poe seemed reluctant to end this game since this woman was of notoriety, and these letters were perhaps a notch in his masculinity.

I showed up at Mr. Poe's in an attempt to aid this woman. When he opened the door and saw me there, he was shocked and appalled that I would attempt such a mission and stick my nose where it didn't belong.

But why, I asked, not return what could be the ruin of one who had made a mistake by engaging with him in the first place? Instead of cooperating, he made a fuss over it, calling me out as a busybody. Upon hearing about this, many eagerly sided with him with their already existing distaste for me as a women's rights advocate.

When all started to spin out of control, this woman's husband stepped in, demanding a retraction from the scorned woman and the letters from Mr. Poe. Seems it required a man to end this scandalous situation.

From there, my relationship with Mr. Poe became strained, but I would do it again to show that women indeed should come to the aid of other women when deliberate manipulation and recklessness abound. Although both women and men knowingly engaged in what could be viewed as reckless behavior, men emerged rather unscathed where women were considered tainted and often ostracized, left with little means to support themselves. Why women should suffer double or more than men did for comparable behavior, I could not witness silently.

Maria

FOR SOMEONE WITH MY INSECURITIES, I WONDERED WHY I was attracted to ladies' men, but then again, I guess it made sense.

It was a pure head game. There he was, the flirt, the smooth-talker, the sweet all the bees were buzzing. I'd put myself right in there. Choose me, choose me. And usually, he would because why not?

There was no talk of feelings. This was a head game, not a heart game. I would be queen of the hill for a while, days, weeks, even months. But the other bees were always buzzing and inevitably, one would be allowed in. It always stung and I was usually speechless. What can one say when there was never anything to say?

Yoni's friend visiting from Israel was a good-looking guy, emanating distinct ladies' man vibes. Yup, I got right in line. And what do you know? He chose me! I visited him in Swampscott where they were working that summer.

I never felt that comfortable with Charlie. He was arrogant and stiff but I tolerated it. It was flattering that he wanted to spend time with me, he wanted to be more than friends with me, he was into me. After all, he was full of intrigue, always wearing black. He looked like a darker-skinned, blacked-haired Paul Newman, his white teeth sparkling. And he was a PI, a private investigator, for heaven's sake.

There was an eerie silence from Theresa and Yoni about my involvement with Charlie. They said nothing about it, and clearly, they wanted nothing to do with it. They didn't discourage; they didn't encourage. They often left us alone, which made sense.

They knew something I didn't know. Charlie was two-timing, and they didn't want to break the news. It wasn't their place to rat Charlie out or to hurt my feelings. It was something they decided to live with, like the weather. What do you do when others engage in such antics?

When I found out, my pride was bruised. I had ignored the signals that Charlie was a snake in the grass because the signals were flashing from the start. It puzzled me that Theresa and Yoni didn't tell me sooner that he was seeing me on weekends and Stacey during the week. But I knew I couldn't blame them. They had been looking after me for years. Their job was done.

Charlie told Yoni that when he was with Stacey, he put a pillow over her face because she was ugly. Such a disturbing image I could not get out of my mind, yet I must admit that I found some consolation in it. It's embarrassing to admit that this type of nonsense threw a pathetic morsel my way.

Margaret

Most of the men I had romantic feelings for, at least earlier on in my life, were men with whom I started out as close friends. Our relationships were built on intellectual connections. Then somewhere along the way, while we shared philosophical thoughts and ideas, I began to care for them as more than a friend. This was not reciprocated, and I began to feel that a romantic relationship may be something I would not experience; perhaps I was to be everything unto myself, and after a while, I resigned myself to such a life. It wasn't my first choice. I, like others, longed to be loved. Even though I had resigned myself years earlier to being bright, if ugly, I still couldn't shake the desire for an intimate relationship.

I was hurt when a close male friend would turn from me to another woman—one not so intellectual, one more delicate, more beautiful. I managed through the pain and disappointment and was able to emerge supportive of the budding relationship, even when the chosen one was one of my close girlfriends.

But it was different with James. We did not begin with an intellectual relationship but one of lightness, enjoying one another's company. We met one evening at a literary soiree, and I was immediately taken by his look—dark hair with blue eyes. James was a banker who had moved here a few years before from

Germany, and this appealed to me since Germany and its writers and culture were near and dear to my heart. James and I enjoyed attending lectures, visiting galleries, and spending time at Turtle Bay, where I was living with the Greeleys. He would bring his dog, Josey, and we'd spend carefree hours roaming the grounds while Josey romped and took a swim in the river.

As is common, others were able to see James in a way I did not. I had never experienced quite this kind of flirtatious attention before and couldn't help but find pleasure in it. Many wondered how I could have written a book such as *Woman in the Nineteenth Century*, where I extolled women not being treated as playthings, warned women to beware of men only out to satisfy their own needs, and here I was, falling for a man such as those I cautioned about. Was I not strong enough, smart enough, independent enough to avoid falling into the arms of such a man or any man at all? Although I mightily believed every word I had written, I was human, and at times, my heart betrayed me.

I desperately wanted to believe James was all he said he was and was not using me to access Horace Greeley and other connections. I was wrong.

When James tried to force a physical connection one day on the banks of the river, I was shocked and pushed him away. This was the first time a man had aggressively made a move on me. Yes, I was progressive but I wasn't reckless. I, too, had been steeped in this culture, one where women had to protect themselves, and ignoring such principles could deem her unworthy. And frankly, I was terrified and somehow knew that this would have to mean so much more to me than him. I pushed him off and, conflicted, regretted it almost immediately. We continued to see one another, but it wasn't the same. There was a coolness and distance in our relations from then on, as though he was punishing me for not giving him what he wanted.

James made plans to go abroad to deal with some issues and to visit his ailing mother. Still holding out hope that we might have a future, all summer long I wrote letters to him. I didn't receive any in return, so I continued to write periodically but held on to the letters, waiting to receive one back from him. That never happened and before long, I heard he was engaged to another, one he had been involved with for quite some time, one he had lied to me about and concocted an entire scenario around, making himself out to look saintly.

Yes, he played me for a fool and left me behind, me and his playful dog, Josey.

Maria

I HAD EMERGED FROM A CONFUSED STATE OF EXISTENCE, from years of being tortured by thoughts and the feelings that followed these thoughts. Thoughts that I was worthless, dumb, fat, and that the world was a dark place where I would never find happiness. I colored mandalas, talked to family and friends, took long, rambling walks, and tried to curb my eating. I daydreamed of a better me. I went to counseling where I was diagnosed with general malaise, which depressed me more. Even my depression wasn't special.

I started to come back to life the final semester of my undergraduate experience. Spending months in Israel on a kibbutz helped me to begin to see myself and appreciate what I had to work with. It helped me muster the determination to complete an English degree on a decent note. From there, with eyes open and not ready to stop, I went on to earn a teaching certification and master's degree. But what ultimately lifted me, what threw me a lifeline, was Henry David Thoreau's *Walden*.

Sitting on the back porch at my parents' house, watching colorful birds at the feeders, gazing at my father's lush garden, and savoring Thoreau's words anchored me: *and not, when I came to die, discover that I had not lived.* No, I thought, that would indeed be a waste. I began to embrace Thoreau's message that nature offers us the key and that quiet and solitude allow us to answer our own questions. I believed that Thoreau, with those sad eyes and slouchy shoulders, was a true friend to me and that his message would forever hold me up in the choppy waters of life. In those moments, I realized I'd rather become more a part of life than leave it. No matter what happened or how I felt, dying was inevitably going to happen one day, and contemplating making it happen sooner was no longer anything I was compelled to do.

Teaching high school English proved more fulfilling than I imagined. I derived satisfaction from introducing topics, including writers, their works and ideas; and witnessing a number of students become genuinely interested and excited. Granted, a larger number couldn't wait for the bell to ring, but still, I was connecting with some of them and it felt positive to have an impact. Another aspect about teaching that appealed to me was having the summer off between school years, and I took my sister-in-law up on her offer to travel Europe.

That summer we traveled a stretch of western Europe. It was primarily a tourist trip, no attempt to mix or get to know anyone who lived there. We hopped the train from country to country, from pension to villa, with our pamphlets and cameras in hand. We were as invisible to those who lived there as they were to us.

Besides Amsterdam, which proved surprisingly amazing, Rome held the most intrigue. After years of Latin in high school—which I took to avoid speaking a second language out loud—I was awestruck by the drive down the Appian Way, the Forum, and the Coliseum. But Rome became a painful place when my sister-in-law announced she was flying back to London for a few days, leaving me alone with her mother, who, having been to Rome before, was not interested in venturing far from the hotel.

I was at a loss because I had been warned about Rome's high crime rate, especially when it came to unsuspecting tourists. I decided my best move was to join group tours to the catacombs and other sites.

Rome continued to darken for me, tainted by wondering the real reason behind Becky's return to London where some friends of hers from college were living. Did my brother know she was in London and not here with us in Rome? I couldn't quite shake a feeling of dread.

Margaret

There was one who would not be as easy to launch as the others. Lloyd, from a young age, presented a new sort of challenge for our family, especially for me, who was charged with providing the educational foundation necessary for the brothers Fuller to enter Harvard. Lloyd didn't so much resist as escape the instruction I imparted. Somehow it rolled off him, and a second dose didn't seem to stick either. I worried and in turn, so did my parents.

It became clear that Lloyd would require an alternate path through life. Unless a suitable situation was established, he would require the eternal shelter of family to provide a buffer from the realities of a world not welcoming to those whose ways and needs were harder to apprehend.

As a supporter of the utopian community Brook Farm and friends with many of its founders, I was able to place Lloyd, then a teen, in the school there. I imagined it would provide a healthy balance of instruction, physical labor, and community—a place that might meet his needs. I was a frequent visitor and speaker on the farm, so I would see Lloyd often, and my connections on the farm would alert me to any concern.

I prayed daily that Lloyd would stay the path, which he did for a while. In true Lloyd style, it soon fell apart, and what once seemed a good situation was no longer. With the search for another position for Lloyd underway, Elizabeth Peabody agreed to hire him to work in her bookshop in Boston. Lloyd assumed this role, and to his credit—not for a lack of trying, his ability to stay the course and fend for himself significantly compromised—he hung in there for a while.

Soon after, while living in New York, I visited the Bloomingdale Insane Asylum and was filled with hope for my youngest brother and others like him. I witnessed that the right circumstances allow what is sound in everyone to surface. This environment provided these patients the correct measure of peace and space to find within themselves a saneness among what is usually considered insane. I was determined that Lloyd, not quite a candidate for the asylum, would find that place too, and his family, especially me, would help him do that.

Maria

I WALKED INTO THE WINDOWLESS TEACHERS' LOUNGE IN the high school and it hit me. I couldn't stay here any longer. Looking at the teachers who had been there for years depressed me. At my age, there was nothing to their lives and attitudes that appealed to me. Some were admittedly hanging on for a few more years to cash in on their retirement, others were only going through the motions. Others actually disliked the students and dreaded going to work in the morning. Thank goodness there were some, both new and veteran, who were there for the right reasons and loved the students and what they did.

That particular morning, the only ones in the lounge were what some of us referred to as "deadwood," those hanging on for the decent retirement package. It hit me like a brick. I was twenty-eight and not ready to settle for twenty-minute lunches in this lounge. I didn't renew my contract when it came time, and although I didn't have another job lined up, I knew it was the right move for me.

I scoured the papers and ran across an interesting ad in the *Boston Globe*. It was for Readak, a company out of Acton, Massachusetts, that trained college graduates to teach reading and study skills courses in private high schools around the country and the world. That sounded adventurous. It wasn't long before I was on my way to Acton for an interview. Seeing as I already had a couple years of teaching under my belt, I was an unusually seasoned candidate, and they readily offered the position. Weeks later, I was packing to move into a Holiday Inn close to the Acton headquarters for four weeks of training, at the end of which we would receive our first placements.

Being cooped up in this hotel enabled me to witness the progress I had made. A few years older than the other trainees, I was able to say no to the parties happening in the other rooms without feeling like I was missing out on anything. I did not feel the need to find a way to fit in or to sulk if I did not. I felt oddly comfortable with myself and genuinely excited about this new direction.

Soon we were packed into a room, being called one by one to hear our placements. As I waited, I prayed for placement in a desirable location. I wanted to leave New England. As others exited after meeting with the director, they announced their eight-week placements and I was not envious of any of them. Then my name was called.

How did I feel about a cross-country trek to Carlsbad, California? At that moment, my world opened up. I was traveling cross-country! I was going to be teaching at a private school on the Pacific Coast! Yes, I had escaped the stale teachers' lounge. I could breathe the fresh air already.

I had much to do to prepare for this trip. My dad, who always supported me no matter what, helped me purchase a new car because no one believed my little beat-up diesel VW Rabbit was up for the drive. And while discussing my venture with my brother and his wife, she offered to accompany me and fly back home once I found a place to live out there. Becky loved to travel and a drive cross-country appealed to her, so she dived into planning our trip. Becky was an incredible excursion planner and I trusted her. She had meticulously planned our trip to Europe the summer before and all had gone well.

It was a chilly late August morning when we loaded up the trunk and threw our sweaters and the Tupperware loaded with homemade muffins on the back seat. We planned to rotate driving shifts and had our route precisely mapped out. Our first stunning sight was the Blue Ridge Mountains as we drove through at sunset.

We arrived at our hotel each evening, sometimes later into the night than others. Ken Burns's Civil War documentary was making its debut, so most nights we settled in after a long day of sight-seeing and driving to catch an episode. In the mornings, we'd make hotel coffee and eat one of the muffins Becky had baked. By the third morning, the muffins were moldy so we were forced to dump the rest of the batch in the trash. Time for more variety.

We took a riverboat cruise down the Tennessee River in Knoxville, conjuring images of Mark Twain, and happily roamed downtown Nashville. After a night in Amarillo in the panhandle of Texas, we rolled into Santa Fe, the city I seriously fell for during the brief time we were there. It was airy and artsy, the sun was warm, not hot. Bathed in a gentle light, colors were more pastel than bold and it buzzed with an energy of creativity. The food we ate was healthier than other travel meals, and the mountains off in the distance made the whole place feel expansive, more open to everything. It was hard to drive away.

After a captivating visit to the Grand Canyon, we finally arrived on the other coast of the United States. To dip our toes in the Pacific Ocean for the first time felt monumental, and to witness a west coast sunset was a real thrill. It didn't hurt that Carlsbad was a quaint seaside town, and knowing we had arrived safely added a splash of relief to the excitement. I was able to secure a room in a house with several other young professionals, and the day I moved in, Becky flew back to Boston.

FOUR

Margaret

CONSIDERING I HAD A LOT TO SHARE AND THE ERA IN which I lived, I became an avid letter writer. The only way to communicate with people I cared about who lived at a distance was to write to them regularly, so this task became prominent in my life, as it was in the lives of so many then. As with all letter writers, receiving them was equally as important. How easy it was to read into the missing letters, the lack of response to the letter you had written from the heart and knew must have been received and read by a particular date. At least you hoped it made it to its intended recipient. And then you'd wait. Sometimes it seemed your letters went into the abyss, but then you would discover they were indeed received but not in the way you had hoped. Depending on the situation, you may have wanted them back, but sometimes they were not returned even when you asked repeatedly. When you sent a letter to someone, it then belonged to them, but if you wanted it back for good reason, you hoped the receiver would oblige.

The feather created a slight breeze as my hand moved across the page. I had become such a pro. Of course, how could one not become adept with the inkwell and quill pen these days? And the seal—the seal stamped hot on the flap of the envelope that guaranteed, for the most part, that your intended recipient would be the first to read your words. My feather would glide across the parchment, leaving its looping design behind. I often mused that I was writing a silvery streak, liquid light from the head and heart to the page.

I was a believer and an adventurer. I did not limit what I believed to what I had learned or what I had been told I should believe. I was connected beyond that to the amazing synchronicity of the layers of life. Oh, yes, this awareness provided great expansiveness in thought and great joy and faith in my life. When one believed only in the mysterious HERE, but not THERE, it became personally limiting, and one was no longer open to all the marvels that offered awesome connections to the cosmos. I did not believe in limits. Ever.

I understood the alternative ways we could be intentional and powerful when it came to healing, communicating, discovering. This was not widely accepted, and I wonder if it will ever be. Some used this against me, to debunk me, make me appear weak and not faithful in the traditional sense. But that didn't stop me. What you believe is what you believe. This will guide you, whatever it is.

When I wrote letters to friends, often I would wear a certain ring with a specific gem on my finger—and for good reason. The sapphire for some, emerald for others. The red carbuncle was my gem, symbolic of the passion that burned in me. This fire within was a gift I possessed that constantly propelled me forward. Carbuncle, known as a garnet, was the fiery stone I claimed as my own—a red-hot coal never extinguished.

Maria

One day, I decided to write a letter to my siblings. Not that it was an old-fashioned thing to do; this was before email. We were all in our twenties and living in various places around the country. I was compelled to ask them some questions. We had grown up in the same house with the same parents, experiencing the same events and day-to-day routines. We all used Dial soap and Colgate toothpaste, Prell shampoo and Tide. But here we were now, all scattered and starting our own lives in our own towns with partners and roommates. What, I inquired, are you using for a toothpaste? And shampoo?

I received interesting and humorous responses, the details of which I don't recall. Growing up, we shared everything, but now the details of our lives and our choices were our own.

We had grown up enjoying all the holidays and traditions: the richness of family on Easter, the Fourth of July, Thanksgiving, and Christmas; egg coloring and cheese pies; the annual trip to the north end of Boston for Easter supplies; the neighborhood patriotic Fourth of July parade, blowing on old trumpets and pounding pans with wooden spoons; fireworks in the park and burgers and dogs on the grill; homemade raviolis on Thanksgiving, along with the traditional fixings; the turkey "skin line" and chocolate pudding pie. And Christmas.

Christmas was in a category all its own. Nothing could top the magic of that winter celebration. It started Thanksgiving night when we were first allowed to play Christmas music; the ultimate anticipation; the warmth and glow of the lights; the thoughts of gifts given and received; the Christmas bazaar in the church basement; the ornaments unpacked year after year, including some Mom had since she was a teenager and those we had made over the years.

No one's ornaments could compete with Aunt Caroline's. Hers were so fragile you barely dared touch them. They were Victorian, ornate, and regal. Her tree, when she finally got around to decorating it, was always one of my favorites, and Christmas Eve at her house with my grandparents (because she always lived with them) was the pinnacle of Christmas magic. All those years of utter excitement, of sharing such rich, loving experiences with family left an indelible mark.

Naturally, it happened that what was most dear could not last. Like a shooting star, it shone bright and faded. It's not that life wasn't still exciting and sweet. It's not that love wasn't still there. It happened that these times passed, along with those most credited with making them happen.

I envisioned my relatives who had passed. Aunt Caroline and Aunt Lucy, my dad's sisters, loomed large. They stood out, not necessarily for anything monumental they did but for who they were, the essence of them. They possessed a distinct presence. Many lamented that Aunt Caroline lived in the past. It was true that she often reminisced, but when she talked about beloved family and events from long ago, her eyes lit up. She summoned it all back.

Margaret

One of my strengths was my voice, inward and outward, compassionate and heartfelt, logical and truthful. I could as easily entertain and hold a room with my words as I could hold a heart, develop confidence, or make a lifelong friend. Weaving from history to current events, universal to local, I could go very big and then pull it very close and intimate.

I could make others think beyond the bounds of what they had ever thought before, inspiring and revelatory, and I was with them for the ride. This was no show, nothing I had rehearsed. It was my gift, to reveal the world in ways that would captivate and transcend. It was the outward expression of my being, of who I was and the vision I embraced.

As a young girl, I didn't have many friends, but as I grew older, I did. I had male friends who found me exceptional and accepted me into their circles, my intellect being viewed as masculine-like. But in my late teens and early twenties, I developed many very strong female friendships. We were closer than any friends I would ever have. They confided in me and me in them. We did not hesitate to share everything and treasured our time together, spending weeks together when we could. This was the biggest reward for my gift, these friends with great trust in me and me in them. This string of friends was like the stars in the heavens.

My ability to express was complemented by my ability to listen, hear, and connect in the place that brings humans closer, as close as they can be—a communion of the souls.

Maria

I BEGAN TO BE KNOWN IN MY FAMILY AS MARIA LETTER. This nickname was not referring to the innocuous letters I sometimes wrote. I wrote a lot of letters to family and friends in general, usually updating them about what I was doing and letting them know how much I cared about them. I suppose even this harmless letter writing was a means to a voice not as well developed in person.

This was especially true when it came to situations of contention. Boy, could I write a letter then. I had a way with my words of indignation and anger. I don't recall many of the letters I wrote from that vantage point, but I wrote enough of them to earn the nickname Maria Letter.

One does stand out, one I wrote to my sister-in-law after she left my brother. I suppose it had been brewing since Rome. My brother wished I hadn't written that letter. He told me she read it over the phone to him.

I was not proud of this reputation—Maria Letter—because I came to understand it was the easy way out when it came to expressing my heightened thoughts and emotions. Later, when I caught myself wanting to write a letter of that sort—one laden with ugly righteousness—and there were many occasions when I composed such letters in my mind—I stopped. If I was not comfortable using my words in person or, minimally, over the phone to voice such sentiments, I no longer permitted myself to write that letter.

Margaret

My abundance of spiritual and intellectual fortitude was not always matched in physical stamina. At times, this was infuriating. Engaged in a mission or two, I would be forced to retreat and take to bed in the stillness of a darkened room. At times, I cursed my physical self, the weaker side of me. Why couldn't it keep up with my ambition, with the numerous tasks I wanted and needed to tend to? How much more could I accomplish, how much faster could I move if only my physical self could maintain a steady pace?

But no. It couldn't. I would begin to feel low on energy, then fretful. Next would be a faint pounding in the head until the crescendo could not be ignored. Time to stop. Time to crawl into myself. To lie still. To settle the mind.

Once I'd resigned myself to where I would be spending the next hours and even days, once I understood that this was bigger and stronger than the other parts of me, I settled in for the excursion. When thoughts came, I examined them patiently and thoroughly. When feelings came, some strong, I let the tears flow. When humorous recollections appeared, I laughed out loud. It was entertaining, cleansing, refreshing and, I'd always discover, much needed.

My body knew what my mind did not, what my emotions ignored; it knew it needed a rest. I never gave it enough credit.

I was lucky to have family and household staff I loved and trusted look in on me, care for me, feed me what my body could tolerate, keep me hydrated, and change my clothes and bedding. It was soothing to be taken care of like a small child again.

When my straining eyes and my overactive brain on a fragile neck needed a reprieve, my physical self lowered the boom with a headache undeniably in control. I was forced to relinquish each time.

Maria

All my health issues centered on my ears and throat, listening and speaking. I'd be a fool not to consider the significance of such clustered maladies.

I had my tonsils removed when I was in kindergarten. This was not an uncommon surgery then. My sister Cecilia had hers out a couple years before me. The doctors hoped removing my tonsils would loosen the fluid in my ears so that my hearing would improve. This surgery left me with the sorest throat I've ever had, the silver lining being that I was served ice cream for breakfast, lunch, and dinner for two days in a row and got to hang out in my sisters' bedroom off the kitchen.

Later in life, my voice started to go, frequently becoming hoarse and sometimes skipping out completely. When it became gravelly, it was my sexy voice, whisper-like and mysterious, but clearly, I had to have it checked out.

The diagnosis—calluses on my vocal cords that developed from holding my jaw a certain way that didn't allow the vocal cords to fully separate when not speaking. This constant friction between them had formed calluses, which got in the way of creating the sounds to vocalize. The treatment—have the calluses scraped off, which sounded worse than it was.

The biggest hitch to this surgery was that I couldn't speak for ten days following the procedure. I was given a keyboard to type what I wanted to say, then I'd hit a button and a digital voice would express my sentiments in robotic sounds. It was so hilarious that my friends drained the batteries playing with it before I was out of surgery. Scribbling my words and needs down on paper was easier than dealing with that contraption except when it came to my young daughter, who couldn't read yet.

After a couple weeks, my voice was back. The procedure had worked like a charm. As advised, I tried to monitor how I held my jaw, to loosen it up occasionally and not hold it so tensely as though trying to hold back a floodgate of unspoken, pent-up thoughts and words.

Adhering to the rule of three, there was another issue: While sitting at a red light, an invisible hand grasped the left top of my head and tightened its hold on my scalp. A creeping sensation then ran down the left side of my body, my face, arm, side, leg, and foot. I sat there stunned, thinking I was having a stroke. Terrified, my heart was thumping hard when the light turned green. I took the first right into the Agway Garden Center.

I let the children out of the van and sat on a cement bench in the garden area while they played around. I tried to regulate my breathing and composure. Very soon I was feeling better and the sensation was gone. I looked up to the sky thinking, OK, that's over. I'm good. We loaded back into the van, the kids not asking why we had stopped.

My doctor speculated it could have been a certain type of migraine that causes stroke-like symptoms, but blood work revealed the culprit—a severely hyperactive thyroid, Grave's Disease. Was that why I constantly felt frazzled, on high alert, couldn't sleep well, and was, alas, thin?

Out of three treatment options, I settled on the radioactive iodine treatment. I knew I wanted to avoid surgery. The day arrived when I stood in front of a suited-up person handing me a pill from a cup. I swallowed this radioactive tablet designed to put my thyroid to rest permanently. This bizarre, yet effective treatment forced me to stay away from my children initially, then at a safe distance for weeks afterward. From then on I would be hypothyroid, my poor thyroid now but a lump in my throat to be monitored annually at medical check-ups.

Margaret

My first role models were the great figures I read and dreamed about, people and characters in books I studied. I'm sure when I was very young, I also looked to the many adults in my life as role models, as examples of ways to be. The closest relationship was with my father. He got into my head at an early age, and I aligned myself with pleasing him first and foremost. He looked to me as his little prodigy.

My mother, on the outside of our relationship, could see clearly what was happening. She was proud of me, but she knew mine was not the usual childhood; mine was an unusual experience, and in some ways, that would be good, in others, not. I always loved my mother in a very gentle, natural way. I never had to try to love her. It was a constant love over the years, one that grew with time. My understanding of her became more and more valuable. She was the person I looked most forward to seeing again on my journey home from Europe.

Ellen Kilshaw was my first true idol though. The first time I met her, I fell deeply in love. I hung on every look, every word. She was beautiful, accomplished, and from a world I'd only read about. And, as with any meaningful role model, she acknowledged me and like clay to a sculptor, set out to help shape me. My parents didn't discourage it, especially my father, who hoped her brand of femininity would rub off on me.

Ellen, in her early twenties, was visiting from England and staying with some neighbors of ours in Cambridge. We came to know her quite well, and my entire family, especially my parents, grew to care for her, naming their next daughter Ellen Kilshaw Fuller.

Ellen visited our house frequently and invited me to spend time out with her and others. She saw great potential in the eight-year-old me, and I naturally gravitated to her maturity and independence. My life became infused with a flutter of exciting engagements. My favorite was when I was invited to walk with Ellen and her companions. How I loved to listen in and play that I was one of them, grown-up and loose in the world. When she had to return home months later, I was devastated. I had lost my first love.

We kept in touch for years by letter, and her impact on my family and me was lasting. We never reconnected and soon our letter writing faded, but when we called my sister by her full name, she was there with us still.

Maria

I WONDERED IF I HAD FINALLY ENCOUNTERED A POSSIBLE mentor. She was intelligent, articulate and so put together, she appeared to sparkle. She was someone who, I believed, could guide me, fairly and wisely. Dianne was positioned at the helm of our department on campus. We were in good hands.

As time went on, it appeared to me she was the type who was going to play it safe. Her game plan for the future seemed to rely on moving herself upward to the beat of a hierarchal drum. When a conflict arose, one that several agreed might be resolved through direct communication, she worked to keep her hands clean, to not rock the boat that could muddy her waters. She said no to a request for mediation.

Meanwhile, my co-worker with whom the conflict had arisen, would hum loudly when in the common area, akin to wearing a bell in the forest, advising me not to come out until the humming ceased. No matter what I was doing in my office, when the humming started, I stopped and listened, hearing what sounded like a tune and tempo driven by guilt and anxiety. At times, this bizarre, loud humming made me want to charge her, to confront her about this nonsense, which I was cautioned not to do. Other times, I wished I never had to lay eyes on her for the rest of my days.

I'll never forget Dianne's words to me when I asked again if something could be done to resolve the issue and clear the air. My once-imagined mentor said, "Let it go, Maria. You have no power where this is concerned." She must have noticed the look of utter shock on my face so she explained, "Listen, some people have a limited capacity. That's all there is to it. We have to work with that."

One quality that initially attracted me to Dianne was her coolness, her apparent detachment from things emotional in the workplace, something I struggled with. Perhaps hers was too much of a desire to not engage, to not risk tarnishing her sparkle, to maintain the professional and political status quo. Instead of taking a stand, whatever it may be, when her staff spoke up, she reminded them that they had no power just in case they had forgotten.

Although I did learn from our exchange (some nuggets were valuable), she was not the mentor I had hoped she would be.

Margaret

WHEN I WAS FIFTEEN, LYDIA MARIA FRANCIS STEPPED INTO my life. It was immediately reassuring that she, too, had chosen to be called by her middle name, Maria. Already a published writer of some renown, I was awed by the success she had achieved by age twenty-two, even more impressive due to her humble beginnings. Although I was a young teen and Maria was in her twenties, I was up for any challenge she presented.

We engaged one another in a scholarly and productive way. We chose particular books to read and spent hours discussing our impressions, thoughts, and opinions about their content and more. This exercise was beneficial, supplying information and building skills we utilized for the rest of our lives.

Maria, on the road ahead of me, provided an invaluable glimpse of what to expect. Her experiences revealed the hardships and detours a woman would most likely encounter once visible. Maria was outspoken, a critic of much around us, a speaker of truth. For this, she paid with her career, readership, and sales taking distinct dips and dives. Even friends and supporters turned on her when they felt she had crossed a line. But she persevered, as

I knew I would, never compromising her beliefs and her fight for freedom and rights for all. She was an incredible mentor, and I was forever grateful for the time and attention she shared with me, the faith she had in me. Maria remained a valued friend and supporter as my life took a similar path.

Maria's marriage, which I observed with fascination, made it difficult to spend much time together. Marrying a well-intentioned man, yet one unable to maintain his footing, required Maria to earn and manage the finances. These tasks, especially as a woman, were a drain on her. There were times she wished she had not married, despite that being rather unacceptable. But clearly, being married or not both delivered disadvantages.

Despite her choices and challenges, I continued to admire Maria as she maintained her position as productive and instrumental in our fight for racial and gender equality in this country, but I did not envy her married status.

As Maria faded from my life, Eliza Farrar, thirty-seven, stepped in. How fortunate I was to have these women willingly take me under their wings, having detected my potential and deciding to guide me in what they believed would be most beneficial. Eliza, an American raised in France and England, married a widowed Harvard professor, a safe choice. He would provide financial security as well as status and a steady stream of social connections. This allowed Eliza to mentor others—me in person and others through her publications.

Eliza's focus was less on me as an intellectual project—this work well underway with no sign of stopping—and more relational, aimed at ways for me to be less off-putting and assertive, but strategically so; ways to work a room without insulting and offending with unrefined manners and unregulated emotion. A part of me bristled at this, but I had begun to recognize the value in this vein of growth.

At eighteen I had emerged from the physically awkward phase of plumpness and poor facial skin. A petite person, I naturally slimmed, and Eliza's advice to my dressmaker and hairdresser complemented these changes. Due to her worldliness and position, Eliza became like a second mother to me, providing what my mother could not, and I was wise enough to see how beneficial this was. I accompanied her on many outings where I learned how to come closer—much closer—to having it all, to stepping into my own light, as much for others as for myself.

These two women, Maria and Eliza, set me more steadily on

the path I was determined to walk. They were always there and as time moved on, I was there for them as well.

Maria

No one wanted to say anything. No one wanted to run for office. No one dared speak up for dread of being told they were wrong or simply dismissed as though they hadn't said anything at all. Two or three women shared the helm with five or six men, but they did little to make the environment less hostile and intimidating to the newcomers in this state association. It seemed to secure their positions, these women had to behave as the men, smug and critical, and for this, I could not blame them. It was clearly how the game was played. When some of the newer women attempted to discuss this dynamic—the intimidation factor and how the men dominated and steered discussions, how a shift in this structure and attitude might help—they were told to stop whining.

I, along with a few other women, attempted to voice that the atmosphere was one of a patriarchal closed club, but we were shut down and discounted, as though our concerns were ridiculous. Clearly, we should have taken a different approach because this one backfired.

Being convinced to run for president of this group when I was not ready didn't help. I was not steady enough but I ran, uncontested of course, because others told me it would be good for me and I believed them. It was hell. I was not at all prepared to lead this group and instead of helping me grow, I allowed it to set me back. Ultimately, it was my decision to run and my lack of confidence made the situation sheer torture. How different it might have been if one seasoned woman had cared to mentor me! I'll never know.

The day I asked, out of blinding nervousness: any abstinences? instead of any abstentions? was the day I inhaled pure humiliation. People laughed, of course, and I felt like I had shown my true colors; I was a total, incompetent idiot. I went back under my rock as soon as I could. What an ineffectual president I was.

When my post ended, relief washed over me, and I sat at future meetings quietly, thankfully watching my presidency fade into the background. As the men in the room babbled on and on at these meetings, one-upping each other for what seemed hours on end, it felt as though there would never be any fresh air in this association. Was this need for verbal nonsense, one diatribe to trump the one before, as exhausting for them as my perpetual lack of self-confidence was for me?

And when it came time for nominations, most people looked down and the threat of "we don't leave this room until someone throws their hat in the ring" was akin to the lions in the Coliseum.

Margaret

I LONGED TO MEET HARRIET MARTINEAU, NOTABLE Englishwoman and writer, when she visited Boston but didn't expect more than that. Yet she decidedly invested in me, spending time and energy exploring the me I might be and even altered her travel plans back to England, thinking I might be along for that trip. It didn't work out for me then, but the gesture on her part meant a lot. It cannot be underestimated, the impact of women investing in one another, even if paths ultimately diverge, as Harriet's and mine did.

No matter the agenda or task at hand, I looked to these women, and they taught me more than they realized. They showed me how to be an independent woman and how to be a leader. Their impact went far beyond what they imagined. When one takes an interest in another, it tells them they're worth it. That sticks and sets them on a nobler path.

In turn, I deliberately became a mentor to many of my students, especially at Greene Street School, and to the women who participated in my Conversations in Boston. In my persistent efforts to press forward, through my publications and columns, I became a guide to thousands of women working to expand their lives, striving for quality, truth, and equality. I was always in search of a beacon and became a steady one myself.

My father had raised me to be a voracious reader, and from these books, I learned much about what it means to be human; what justice, fairness, and beauty mean; and what the meaning of life might be. But from these women, I learned self-worth, true strength, and how to present myself as a strong, intelligent woman in a world that didn't value such. They provided me a roadmap where I had none. I'm not sure they thought I would take it as far as I did, but they provided the springboard to my success.

As girls, we were convinced that our main goal was to be chosen by a man—preferably a good man—and that meant a man of some wealth and status, a man with a good name. So here we were, at the gate, elbowing each other for the best position to attract that man our family would approve of and be proud of us for marrying. It became a popularity contest and a beauty contest, with some luck thrown in there too. For even if you were not that beautiful by cultural standards and were not that pleasant, if your family was wealthy and you were lucky enough to be born into it, your chances of being chosen increased, even though you did not possess the looks and talents of other young women.

It was a game and a gamble that took you away from yourself because you were basically being bought and sold, no matter how they tried to package it. Much of our energy went into doing what we could and what we were told to do to secure a man who would then be our end-all and be-all. We had no other rights.

I was born without great looks and into a family with few resources. Although my father was a Harvard-educated lawyer who ended up in politics, in the end, we didn't have a lot when his time in Washington was up and he moved us to a more rural area. But I didn't work to make myself more marketable to men. That was not my aim. I won't lie and say it wasn't important to me; I too wanted a relationship, a partner. But mine would have to be different for I was not able to be submissive in any relationship, be it with a woman or a man.

I thrived on relationships. Humans need other humans for so many reasons—basic survival and enjoyment and learning about oneself. I treasured my friendships with my girlfriends and the women I met along the way. Women often received the message that these relationships were secondary to that one central relationship with their husbands, but these relationships were often more fulfilling, supportive, and exciting than the others. Sharing intimacies, such as fears and goals you would not utter to anyone else . . . what safer place to do that than within a trusted friendship, of which I had many.

Early on, girls realized they were in some sort of competition with one another. That may be why sisterhood was so hard to find, whereas brotherhood seemed more prevalent. We did not trust one another because, well, we could not be trusted. We often took information that was less than complimentary and spread it with the intention that somehow it would take the other woman down a notch. In the back of our minds, consciously or unconsciously, that helped our chances—unless, of course, someone was out there doing that to us too. These types of games were easy to play, especially when we did not know or care about the other person and we were but acquaintances. But when you are a true friend to another woman, you know this person's heart and soul. You could not do that to her, and she could not do that to you. You wished her nothing but sincere happiness and she the same for you. It paid to cultivate true relationships with other women.

To further our rights and create a culture where women were treated fairly and granted the rights men had, we were going to have to come together. No, we did not want more rights than men, and no, we did not want different rights than men. We wanted equal rights. What they had we too deserved.

Maria

When I returned from Europe, I wanted very much to live a different life. I was under the spell of the European lifestyle—one of lightness and liveliness, one of both the contemporary and historical, one of art and beauty. I dreamed of capturing and experiencing that romance and exuberance in my life at home.

Once back, I was excited to pick up with a faltering relationship that I was sure we could make good. I envisioned making a new home with Matt, with classical music and lace curtains. Not like the apartment we had when we lived together previously. That one was not homey, not cozy, and did not signify a real commitment. I was ready to dig in, to make our life together the one I wanted.

Sitting on the front steps at my parents' house not long after my return, he told me he had rekindled with his former girlfriend. He was sorry, but no, our relationship was over. I remember crashing. All I had envisioned collapsed. The lace curtains vanished, the artwork on the walls disappeared. A strange nothingness moved in. With this disappointment came the need to rebuild.

Before starting my second year of high school teaching, since my former relationship was irreparable, I accepted an arrangement to move into a house closer to the school with another teacher. This house was out in the country, in a rural section of New Hampshire.

I would move in first, and my roommate, Peter, would arrive a week or so later.

This setting did much to soothe my hurt feelings. It was on a dirt road with an ideal walking route, and the owners had left their dog, Jessie, a golden retriever—a perfect walking companion.

Oh, and my new roommate, Peter? He was a notorious ladies' man.

Margaret

UNDERSTANDABLY, IN SOCIETY AS STRUCTURED, TO A VERY great extent, men became women's ambition. And I suppose in this same society, it made sense that many men extracted a thrill from playing with women's lives. Like kids in a candy store, some could not stop themselves from procuring more than their share, creating ridiculous circuses for themselves like the scenario with Mr. Poe and his married love interest, not wanting to let go even when its time was up. How to reject the advances, the flirting, the sweetness that seems yours for the taking?

My James, not able to sacrifice one woman's attachment to secure another's—mine. How complicated the day where two or three or even more women are demanding your affection, your confidences, your money. How much of a bind many found themselves in, living in the topsy-turvy world stamped by patriarchy.

When I discovered that the woman living with James was not a poor, lost soul he had rescued but was his mistress, I was shocked. Although my original reaction when he told me about her consisted of anger and abhorrence, I later decided to trust and believe him. I believed him to be a kind and noble man, one who would, of course, do this for another in dire need. I even set out to find others he could contact to help this unfortunate woman secure proper employment and a more permanent living arrangement. I was not able to believe James would have another woman living with him while courting me. I later wondered what she was thinking. What did he tell her, and did she believe in him as much as I did?

If access to my connections was his aim, thankfully few, if any, took. This spared me hearing of him as I progressed in my busy, increasingly productive life.

Maria

I HAD BEEN THE OTHER WOMAN AND THE VICTIM OF THE other woman several times in my life, not where marriage was involved but hurtful just the same.

I had two-timed on my boyfriend in high school. Standing on the back porch that Sunday afternoon when he found out and punched the post so hard his knuckles bled, I was speechless. I felt his pain, both in his heart and throbbing knuckles. To think that I had acted in such a way only to prove I was more desirable than Sally! It was careless behavior that had nothing to do with how I felt about the boy. It was more a jostling for position with my female peers.

I was single and in my early thirties when a married student in our Adult Learner Program made a move on me. I was surprised when he showed up at my apartment bearing cough drops and cough syrup when I was sick. On the one hand, how thoughtful; on the other, I knew this was crossing a line. I didn't let him in, knowing I shouldn't.

Weeks later in my office, he was much clearer about his interest. Did I feel the same? I looked at him and all I could see was his wife. All I could feel was awful for her. What if she knew her husband was sitting in an office across from his English instructor, expressing such desire? "I would never do that to your wife," were the words that tumbled from my mouth. What a rush. I was flooded with a sense of respect, a sense of doing what was right, a sense of power to disentangle such behaviors.

Maybe it was being a mother, a mother of a daughter. Maybe it was disgust at a man setting out to cheat on his wife. Maybe it was me realizing that he thought I would do such a thing. Wherever the wires had crossed and wherever my resolve sprang from, I was consciously done engaging in such activities.

Margaret

WHEN I LATER DISCOVERED JAMES WAS ENGAGED TO BE married, part of me burned with betrayal and foolishness all over again, but a greater part of me was released. I implored him to return the letters I had written to him over the months we had been involved. He agreed to this request but never followed through. They were later be published for all the world to read.

An opportunity to visit Europe had resurfaced. My first chance had been thwarted by the untimely death of my father and the ensuing responsibilities and financial difficulties that came my way. Now, years later, when writing for the *New York Tribune*, I was offered a chance again due to the generosity of some friends, which involved me tutoring their son along the way and an agreement from Horace Greeley to continue producing my column from Europe. With letters of introduction from Waldo, I would have a chance to meet literary and social counterparts. Others needed no letter of introduction, based on the popularity of my book *Woman in the Nineteenth Century*, which paved the way.

I never reconnected with James, and by then it didn't faze me, for those I was able to connect with were some I thought I may never have the chance to meet—William Wordsworth and George Sand being two I was especially eager to encounter.

In a bold move, I showed up at George Sand's house unannounced. Having been intrigued by her for years, I could not stand the thought of missing an opportunity to meet her while in France. I approached her house and knocked on the door. The keeper answered and left to announce my arrival and soon she approached, dressed so feminine-like, not in her usual men's attire. I fear my face revealed my shock. This supported my writing, in *Woman in the Nineteenth Century*, of my belief in the fluidity of gender, masculinity and femininity coursing through each one of us, no need to be locked in one or the other. We engaged in poignant conversation, despite my not-so-good French. This was one of the highlights of my trip by far.

While in Paris, I also had the pleasure of meeting Adam Mickiewicz, and he put any feelings I still held for James Nathan to rest once and for all. Where James was a phony, Adam was purposeful and authentic. We had a deep, immediate connection that may have been more if our paths were more closely aligned, but I do credit him for helping to set me free.

Maria

He was a three-season athlete, truly outstanding in all—soccer, baseball, and hockey. Although he was a year behind me in high school, I was comfortable in our relationship.

We met when he was in the school play, which my friends and I were always a part of. His involvement, along with the involvement of several of his friends, was coerced. The drama club director was the father of one of his friends and this particular play called for more guys than normally joined the drama club productions. They were persuaded to help the director out, plus, even though they had to wear tights, they got to wear armor and carry swords, so it wasn't that bad.

I don't recall if it was a ring or a bracelet he made me out of scraps of wire, but it was sweet, and from there we dated for quite some time. Our biggest obstacle was John's height. I wasn't taller than him but I was pretty much the same height. On a day-to-day basis, this was OK, but certain things made me a little taller, and this was not OK.

It bothered him when I let my hair go naturally curly. In the seventies, curly hair on a white woman was not considered fashionable, so normally, after I washed my hair, I would pull it back as tight as I could in a ponytail, which we called a "Ben" since it resembled Ben Franklin's. This all changed in high school when round brushes and blow dryers made their way into our house. I could blow-dry my hair while constantly running the brush through it, which helped tame it and framed my face with hair feathers.

Yet now and then I felt like letting my hair go, and those days posed a problem for John, the perfect scholar-athlete in his Izod polo shirt, collar up. My wild hair made me a little taller than him. This was but one of our issues. The '70s espoused platform sandals, and I did love mine. But they made me taller than him, so I didn't wear them as much as I wanted. Days when I let my hair go free and wore my platforms were not the best for our flimsy relationship. John met me hesitantly after class and walked a bit ahead or behind me, just in case.

Then came prom. Of course, I did not intend to let my hair loose on prom night, but the platforms became an issue. I planned to wear them as I needed the height with my gown. But this bothered John. I could not be taller than him on the dance floor and in photos, he pleaded. The pinnacle of this conundrum was when he arrived at my door that afternoon with several pairs of his mother's flat white sandals, which I refused to consider. I would not go to those lengths to appease his need to be taller, even though I could see where he was coming from; me being taller challenged his masculinity, his place of dominance. Being a short man in this society was already hard on him, and he made up for that through his incredible athleticism. Me and my platforms, although seemingly harmless, called into question much of this insanity.

If only I'd suggested that John wear heels that night. That would have been a good solution.

Margaret

I'll admit I was an intense individual. I usually wanted more—more depth, more truth in conversation. I craved more substance in friendship. I wanted more from myself and I often demanded more from the world. This could be construed as me being needy, me being romantically interested where I wasn't. Yes, I may have wanted a deepening of our relations but not always a physical one. There are various kinds of intimacies. I wasn't afraid to ask others for what I wanted and needed, especially when I knew they had it to give.

I had some very intense friendships with both women and men. At times, I did want more from some of the relationships in my life, but that was to be expected, right? Why shouldn't I have felt those pangs? Why shouldn't I have felt such desires? I wasn't the one who was looking for intimacy to interfere with marriage. It was usually the married one who did that, for the married one was often the unhappy one.

On many occasions, I shared a bed with close girlfriends. We were involved, sharing secrets, desires, hopes, and dreams deep into the night. Some of my best days and nights were spent in intimacy with these precious friends, especially my lifelong friends, Cary and Anna.

It's also true I wanted more from my close friend Waldo. There was a barrier about him that kept all his relationships, even his wife, Lidian, at arm's length. This barrier kept him in charge and barricaded his true heart and soul from even his closest companions. I longed to shatter that barricade! I wanted to do that for him and for me. I never wanted a one-way street. I was in no way a taker who sought only attention and didn't lavish it on the other person.

Yet I was accused of that. I was labeled as "needy" for desiring authentic relationships, ones that broke the prescribed boundaries, ones where we could bare our souls, speak our darkest fears and our brightest hopes and desires. I wanted to banish the shame and fear of exposing our most human selves. I wanted to rise to great heights in my friendships, to reach new levels of purity and honesty. I always believed in the quest for self-improvement—perfection even—and this was true for my relationships too. I never was able to achieve what I considered a truly pure and complete relationship with either a man or a woman in my lifetime, but I came close.

Maria

I STRUGGLED TO IMAGINE WHAT THEY WERE LIKE WHEN they were home alone in their houses, living their lives. My mother's family. Those stoic Yankees, those farmers from New Hampshire. Those living by the credo *No one said life would be easy. No one said life would be fair.* On this side of my family, things were cut and dried. Gatherings were short and sweet and when they were over, they were over. No sitting around sipping on strong coffee and homemade wine, discussing the issues of the day or the past. Especially the past. Why discuss the past, silly, it's over. There's nothing you can do about it.

From my perspective, it seemed no frivolous thing was allowed or dwelled upon. What did they discuss, the adults around the table? What mattered to them? Certainly, emotions were not readily welcomed. This trickled down to our household with my mother's consistent reminder that nobody wanted to see you cry, so go to your room. Or "If you're going to cry, I'll give you something to cry about," meaning that feeling sad or upset was not a good enough reason to cry.

As a child, my mother's mother seemed mean. But I don't think she really was. It was the no-nonsense aura she exuded—figure-it-out, buck-up, and hide behind the shed until you get yourself together. It was survival mode, I guess. Because life wasn't easy. Life wasn't fair. And if it was this way for me, what makes me think it will be different for you? Do I want better for you? Perhaps, but I'm not going to wish it or project it because it may not happen.

These grandparents would invite us for sleepovers now and then. Their house was appealing because it offered more tangibly fun things, and they had more resources than my other grandparents, the Italian ones. There was a big, hilly yard a bit out of town with a duck pond and lots of mica to discover and peel. There were chickens and a swinging hammock that would occupy us for hours. There was a finished basement where we could play without disturbing the adults.

The night my sister Theresa and I, along with a couple of girl cousins our age, were chosen to sleep over was an exciting one. We had time to play, then dinner, and watching TV before bed. It was then I realized I had forgotten to pack my pajamas. This realization terrified me because what would my big bad grandmother say? What would she do, towering over me with that serious gaze, her cat-eye glasses, her lack of patience with such foolishness?

"I forgot to pack my pajamas," I uttered as the others scampered off to change.

She briefly studied me, no frown, no smile, just a steadiness. She walked down the hallway toward her room and returned with a nightgown of her own. She took the scissors and cut the length from the hem and arms. "Here you go," she said, handing it to me. My sister and cousins chuckled seeing me in Gram's altered nightdress. I felt a little embarrassed but more relieved that I had not been scolded.

Secretly, I felt honored to be wearing one of Gram's nightgowns. I left it in her bedroom the next morning and wondered if she would hang on to it for the next time a granddaughter was as foolish as me.

Margaret

When Father was away in Washington, which was often and for long stretches of time, my mother's sisters would stay with us. These were fun and loving times that brought my mother great joy. We children received a heavy dose of caring, one my mother was not able to confer on all of us by herself.

There was chatter and laughter and a bond I had never seen before. The sister bond. The knowing that comes from growing up together and from being female. It was like they knew what the other was thinking and would recite phrases together with great merriment. They would laugh at things we children could not understand, and they would work with a synchronicity you could tell was years in the making. It was an experience of beauty and comfort.

These women were capable of the incredible when they worked together, and even at my young age, I marveled at that. It was unfortunate that they were often separated from one another at a rather early age, traded off to men who kept them in their domestic castles and slowly diminished the bonds formed through years of family and friendships.

Soon they did not know each other as well, and soon they did not work together on much of anything but maybe one or two days a year. How much was forfeited? What took the place of these incredible bonds was often distrust. Now they were beholden to one man and one man only, and he had the power. He came between them whether he intended to or not.

When my father left politics and didn't go away anymore, especially after we moved to Groton, my mother's sisters stopped coming to stay at the house with us, and we lost those special times. I missed them dearly. My relationship with my aunts would have been so much better if my father hadn't been in the way.

Over time I discovered that women often lacked cohesiveness, especially when we needed one another most. When it looked like we were doing well, we appeared to be a threat. It was lonely at the top for women because we had been conditioned to make it that way. It was even more lonely for women at the bottom.

Times like these I longed for my sister Julia Adelaide and wished there were not so many years and brothers between me and Ellen. But I had women friends, many of them, and we were starting a fire—one that would continue to burn long after I was gone.

Maria

As we got older, Gram's tone toward us grew more bitter. We started to call her biting remarks Grammy Ball Digs or GBDs for short. They were sharp comments designed to cut, the lash causing us to burn since it was not permissible to speak up or back. Perhaps they were aimed more at our parents, my dad being one Gram and Grampa didn't initially approve of.

Our going to college seemed to be a sore spot. If one of us dropped a spoon or didn't know the answer to a question, we were met with Gram's, "Is that what they teach you in college?"

It seemed Gram thought college a frivolous or ridiculous thing to do, the cost of it outweighing the benefits. Because her life was, especially early on, one of labor and practicality. Something as loosey-goosey as a liberal arts education or college seemed indulgent, unnecessary. Look at Grampa, with an elementary school education and very successful with his own excavation company.

The philosophical and lifestyle differences between my mother's and father's families were extreme, and I often found myself favoring my father's side, the Italians, with their seemingly more tolerant and unconditionally loving approach, and their love of art, opera, and the unseen.

But I came to understand and value my mother's family's strength and heartiness, their "get up and get it done" attitude, especially as both grandparents on that side mellowed, moved closer to center, expressed their love more openly, and welcomed their "black sheep" son-in-law, my father, into the fold.

Margaret

When my travel companions, the Springs, decided it was time to head back to America, I was not ready to go. After experiencing an exhilarating liberation from the constraints of my country—one I had never felt before—I did not want to return. Not yet. During our travels, I had met so many celebrated people, two of whom had stoked the fire in me. I was not ready to risk having this doused upon my return to New England.

One of these men, Giuseppe Mazzini, I met in London while he was in exile for his prior revolutionary involvement. Knowing of him already, it was monumental to encounter this larger-than-life figure in person. His spirit, his single-minded goal of independence for his people, connected with me. His fight was a noble one, and he was a noble man who would be called on again to march for his country's unification and liberation.

Mazzini was running a school for illiterate Italian boys, those who spent their days on the streets. When he asked me to address these boys, there was no way I would decline. Staring into their curious yet suspicious eyes, I did my best to impart my genuine compassion and hope for their futures in England, but more vehemently for their eventual return to Italy.

Leaving Mazzini behind was difficult. There was a powerful,

natural connection and much I stood to learn from him, but knowing in my heart we'd meet again on Italian soil made it easier.

In Paris, I had the distinct opportunity to meet Adam Mickiewicz, a poet and professor exiled from Poland due to his radical ways. This included a break with the established church, similar to Waldo back home. Yet, comparing Mickiewicz to Waldo only went so far. Mickiewicz embodied it all—great intellect and passion visible in his eyes, his words, his every move. Mickiewicz matched me in intensity and outmatched me in bodily passion, boldly asking if I planned to remain a virgin. To be asked such and to engage in this talk brought me close to fainting, literally. He lived a much freer, openly liberal life, as did others in Paris.

Mickiewicz's inquisition set me thinking, stoking another sort of fire. I found myself revisiting my commitment to never engage in what I labeled an earthly union.

After saying goodbye to the Springs in France, I made my way back to Italy and eventually settled in Rome. Winds of rebellion stirred the air, and I could tell I was in for an experience I never imagined I'd encounter. I continued my columns for the *Tribune*, critiquing culture, art, and literature, but also keeping my fellow Americans updated on what was developing in Italy. I knew it was going to be big, and I wanted as much support from my home country as possible. A legitimate struggle for independence was always one to get behind, and who should know that better than the United States?

Maria

As we went from country to country, city to city, sight-seeing, scoffing up souvenirs, and dining out, I became more and more restless. This especially hit me in Italy, where Becky and I spent hours in the art museums in Florence. Being an artist herself, Becky would set up her easel and sketch what she saw. Me, I would stare with amazement, especially at art pieces I had studied in my art history courses in college. Leaving Becky behind, I'd work my way through entire galleries, coming out the other end with a need to cease looking at the world as though window shopping and to start participating as some sort of creator myself. I was feeling the distinct need to do something, to be engaged in some way—any way—at this point.

I fantasized about making lace curtains. I'd never liked sewing. It gave me an immediate neck ache. All I had ever sewn were some oddly shaped stuffed animals and in middle school, an angel top—a shirt with sleeves like wings. Yet I felt this intense desire to redecorate my apartment when I returned home, and handmade curtains seemed like a good place to start since I coveted the dreamy, airy, lacy ones fluttering in the tall open windows in western Europe.

I decided I wanted my place to be less utilitarian and more aesthetically pleasing. Life was meant to be savored. This was why my Italian grandmother's house appealed to me. It had a rich, captivating feel with statues in the corners and faded paintings of intriguing landscapes on the walls. Since it was clear I was not going to mix with the locals in Italy, I wanted to step back into my own life and recreate this ethereal feel, embroidered with timeless beauty.

When I arrived back home, I was pumped to live differently, to imbue my life with more color, beauty, and zest—not only my surroundings, but who I was. I moved into a house closer to the high school where I was teaching and did indeed step up my game, but not in ways I had hoped would feed my soul. Those elements continued to elude me.

Margaret

I KNEW I HAD MADE THE RIGHT DECISION TO STAY. I FELT AT home in Italy, more accepted, more alive than ever. Drawn into the Roman Revolution of 1848, I was reminded daily of my country's earlier struggle. I stayed and became, without setting it as a goal, the first female foreign correspondent and war correspondent. Little did I know that not only would I become engrossed in Italy's fight for independence, but I would meet a man who would become the father of the baby I never expected to have. Angelino, little Nino.

Necessary secrecy kept us from openly sharing what transpired between us following our chance meeting in St. Peter's a year earlier. Giovanni was a good-looking man with blue eyes that spoke to my heart. He was kind and unassuming. He cared about me for who I was, not what I had accomplished or my many connections. With him, I felt liberated and allowed myself to go with my feelings. Yet had it not been for the baby, I'm not sure I would have continued our encounter, let alone marry this man. This I would never know.

Aside from Giovanni and an attendant, I was alone when I birthed Nino in the mountains of Rieti. When I had to remove myself from covering the fight and retreat to the mountains, I was fearful—fearful I would die. But the moment was most precious when I held newborn Nino in my arms with Giovanni by my side. No one knew—not my mother, my sister, my brothers, nor any of my very good friends. This was a huge secret.

Soon I returned to Rome to continue my coverage, where Giovanni was stationed all along. Nino stayed back with a wet nurse and caretaker.

Maria

I WAS BORN WITH A BIRTHMARK ON MY LEFT ELBOW. It looked like someone had taken a paintbrush, dipped it in brown paint, and tested it out on my skin. I wished I could get rid of it. I imagined falling on the pavement and scraping my elbow so badly it would remove that ugly brown mark. I wondered, could it be surgically removed?

When I had to wear short sleeves, I'd stand with my right hand behind my back, clasping my left elbow, but after a while that pose would become tiring. Most people didn't say anything about it even though their double-takes showed they'd noticed it.

My mother tried to convince me it was not a birthmark but a beauty mark. That was sweet of her. And when that didn't placate me, and she became frustrated with my pity party, she'd say, *At least it isn't on your face.* That usually shut me up.

The only time my birthmark seemed useful was when I completed the paperwork for my passport, and it asked for an identifying mark. Yes, I have an identifying mark, a birthmark on my left elbow that resembles the negligent stroke of a paintbrush. What I most despised was my most remarkable physical aspect, something that might help identify me in the case of a disaster. Seemed important as I headed to Israel.

To their credit, they let me go. Well, at this point they basically let me do anything I wanted to do. My parents rarely said no, except when we were younger and they had a reason to say no. But as we grew, and especially once we graduated high school, they were not restrictive and did not attempt to control our decisions.

When I announced I was flying to Israel on a one-way ticket because it was all I could afford, they didn't insist I not go. Yet they did try to discourage me, and one way was to inform me they would not drive me to the airport. That was an easy go-around; I had friends.

It wasn't like I was totally jumping into the abyss. My sister Theresa and her boyfriend, Yoni, who was from Israel, were there. I'd overlap with them for a week or two before checking in at the kibbutz. I was signed on as a volunteer at Lahav, a kibbutz Yoni had stayed at while in the army. He would introduce me to people there, especially Ronnie and Annie, who were like second parents to him.

In my lavender Gloria Stevens Figure Salon cap-sleeve shirt, dark purple shorts, and white high-top Reeboks, I appeared to leap from the bright pink aerobics carpet directly onto this secluded kibbutz in the Negev Desert. I resembled the female figures we used to clip from women's magazines—one-dimensional, frozen in a pose. I declined to wear the uniform of the kibbutz—the work clothes, all faded blues. I especially rejected the hat. No hats for me, even in the extreme temperatures of the desert.

At this point, I had pretty much perfected the art of escape. No matter where I was, I could be somewhere else. I could and would transport myself elsewhere. The opposite of being in the moment, whenever possible, I disappeared. I dwelled in a nebulous future because I wanted out. Unhappy with myself, I refused to settle for now.

I escaped in the afternoons at the pool with the other volunteers where, after swimming my laps, I'd settle in the sun with my headphones and daydream while the others laughed and goofed off with one another.

In the evening before dinner, when others would play volleyball, I'd pull on my Reeboks and walk the squeaky-dry roads of the orchards, listening to music that transported me from this place to imagining a future self, one who was much more captivating. I never saw beyond that, didn't drill down to see what that new me was really about. The details didn't seem important. The thrill of escape was what mattered. I kept my distance and although not the healthiest approach, the sanctuary and hope it provided was, in its strange way, sustaining.

Margaret

I gave so much in my life. Due to circumstances, it was who I had become. For this, at times I was taken advantage of, as when I didn't get paid for my work as editor of *The Dial* and for teaching at Temple School in Boston. Neither of these situations compensated me, compounding my perpetual financial woes. Had I been a man, I would have been paid. I would have been taken more seriously when I demanded such.

I moved on knowing that although I didn't get paid monetarily, I had made connections and learned much. Ultimately, I was able to build upon these situations. Teaching at Temple School led to me being hired at Greene Street School in Rhode Island, where I was indeed paid well and where I left my mark on many. My editorship at *The Dial* allowed me to publish a lengthy essay that led to a groundbreaking book and me being hired by Horace Greeley. None of this makes it OK that I was taken advantage of, but for my sanity, it was important to recognize that neither situation was a waste of my time, talent, or energy.

But these situations, along with my uncle's unwillingness to protect us financially, even with my father's money, contributed to a constant struggle, Finally, needing to sell the farmhouse in Groton, we were essentially homeless. I would never have a true home again.

Swimming against the current and keeping my head above water was exhausting and I waged a constant battle in my mind, fighting to stay afloat and to seize any opportunity for me to offer the world what I knew I possessed and, hopefully, be compensated along the way. Through this constant show of courage, I rallied from deep within. Through this tireless stoking of the fire, I propelled myself forward, and this momentum carried others along as well. It was both daunting and amazing, and I would not let up.

When my only option, due to limited money, was to secure our passage back to the United States by cargo ship, I booked it. This fateful decision, one that stirred visions of disaster, seemed my only choice at the time. I could have solicited more help to pay for our voyage home by passenger vessel, but it seemed important that I hold my head high amid so much disapproval. I had to manage this on my own, and this ultimately played into the end of the life we had only begun to create together—me, Giovanni, and Nino.

Maria

My Maria Letter voice was one of judgment, of me expressing disapproval and criticism—something I myself couldn't take. If anyone had written me a Maria Letter, I would have crumbled.

I was most confident when I was admired, looked up to, had something others didn't have. That was my ammo, to feel like, in some way, I was better than others or at least on par with them. When I no longer held that position, I withdrew and decided not to play anymore.

When I imagined my future, whether dreaming or more logically calculating, I didn't envision a wedding, didn't imagine children, didn't imagine any particular career. But I did come to crave a house, pleasantly decorated, with all the essentials.

After high school, early on in my college days when I started to flounder and feel unanchored, I was drawn to paintings and figurines of cottages with warm yellow light emanating from the windows, Thomas Kincaid-type paintings, and other cozy images. It followed that people started to give me house décor and ornaments, especially my mother, who gifted me annually with the Hallmark house ornament of the year. They were adorable—a detailed exterior and an open, even more detailed interior of each room on the flip side. I loved these ornaments and still have the entire collection. These houses seemed like inviting, safe havens and I longed for one. Adrift, unsure, and often melancholy, a home seemed the perfect antidote.

Years later, I started dating a man who collected houses—the real things. He was good at finding a deal on a house that needed tender loving care, and he had vision, not only for how they could be renovated but for the security and comfort they could offer others.

Margaret

Not long after they married, Nathaniel and Sophia Hawthorne moved into a house just down the road from Waldo and Lidian Emerson, with whom I often spent weeks at a time. We were all delighted with the arrangement.

Nathaniel Hawthorne was a writer who was beginning to make

a name for himself, and I was more than pleased to help him along the way by genuinely praising his works as worthy of note, an up-and-coming true American author. I had known Sophia, his wife, for years. She was the youngest sister of Elizabeth Peabody, who lived in Boston and ran an international bookstore and printing press where she hosted many meetings of the minds.

Elizabeth and I had several connections, one being that she taught for Bronson Alcott at his Temple School before I took over the post. She welcomed me into her press to publish the transcendental journal, *The Dial*. So supportive was Elizabeth that she allowed me to hold my Conversations for women at her place as well.

Elizabeth was an entrepreneurial woman, one who kept a low profile, knowing that being a woman was not good for business. She used the pseudonym E. P. Peabody to keep her gender unknown and her business flourishing. She met Nathaniel Hawthorne first and there seemed to be a budding romance there, and Elizabeth seemed willing to promote Nathaniel's work. But a woman like Elizabeth would not do for Nathaniel. He preferred a woman who worked for him, not an independent, entrepreneurial woman serving the greater good.

Sophia and I were well acquainted. She attended the Conversations series I held at her sister's shop and showed herself to be a talented artist, one who could sketch and paint exceedingly well. Sophia and I shared something else in common—debilitating headaches. We were prone to wretched episodes that would take us down for days. I do believe her affliction was worse than mine, more difficult to power through.

When I entered the Hawthornes' new home after their union as husband and wife, I was inspired. Theirs was a marriage that gave me hope—hope that there could exist mutual respect and admiration and a level of equity rarely seen. They were two artists who supported one another's work and who adored each other; a happier, more fair union I had yet to personally witness. Our visits were always joyous. Long, rambling walks and talks, simple but hearty meals, and comforting tea times. I felt so welcomed, even treated like royalty.

Soon a shift took place, especially after the arrival of their first child. Sophia put away her painting supplies, packed away her talents and passion. She retreated into the women's sphere, focusing solely on running their household, raising their children, and attending to her husband's needs.

This shift in their relations, orchestrated by Nathaniel, dowsed our friendship. Over time, I went from confidante to adversary. Although I remained supportive, Nathaniel did not. Sophia followed suit, especially after my book *Woman in the Nineteenth Century* was published. She openly exclaimed to others that I did not know my place, that because I was not married, I had no right or basis to write about marriage and domestic affairs. Once a friend of Sophia's, she now mocked me as "Queen Margaret."

Having relocated to New York City and writing steady columns for the *New York Tribune*, I wasn't of the mind or in the position to attempt amends or to respond to what I heard was said about me. Their remarks stunned and puzzled me, but my life was elsewhere now.

I didn't believe that they didn't care for me, but rather that their reaction was rooted in them being threatened by me as a woman on a mission for change. Although theirs initially appeared to be a marriage of greater equality, in the end, it was not. Behind the scenes, Nathaniel had worked to manipulate Sophia from the start, convincing her that she was his "little dove." He worked exceedingly hard to coerce her into playing a support role for him, and finally, she was convinced that such an arrangement was best.

As I made choices to live my life more freely and unconventionally, they became uncomfortable with me. I was a threat to their arrangement. Honestly, though, I was not the only one they disdained. They burned bridges with many of those who challenged them in any way, Sophia consistently taking her cue from Nathaniel.

As was often the case, Nathaniel was ill-prepared to handle our unusual relationship, one that attracted and repulsed him. Ultimately, he worked me and other women like me into his novels. Maybe I wasn't the only inspiration for Hester Prynne in *The Scarlet Letter,* but I most definitely contributed to the creation of that heroine. It seems I was the model for Zenobia in *The Blithedale Romance*, as well. The suicide in store for Zenobia was indicative of what the author believed I deserved through my bold pursuit for equality and the way I lived my life.

I may have died tragically, but Nathaniel Hawthorne and Edgar Allan Poe couldn't escape their tragic deaths. Poe's was more well known as he was found incoherent in the street one morning in someone else's clothing, the cause not confirmed but perhaps a cover-up of some sort. Hawthorne's tragic passing was subtler. He died as he preferred to live—secluded. Away with his best friend, the unfavorable Franklin Pierce—a man who upheld slavery and was a terrible president—in his room one night, haunted by so much, Nathaniel passed.

FIVE

Maria

While teaching at a private school in Carlsbad, California, and catching up on all the classics I'd missed reading earlier on, life was fulfilling and I felt freer than ever.

One night I agreed to go out with my temporary roommates and their friends. I would rather have stayed in and read but finally caved in to a night out. While sitting at the bar, a friend of my roommates' was sitting a little too close, complimenting me a bit too much. One comment stayed with me—his observation of the small gold cross around my neck, the cross my sister-in-law bought for me on the Ponte Vecchio in Florence the year before. I loved that little gold cross, though I had originally resented that Becky bought it for me because she felt bad that I couldn't afford to buy something for myself. But I loved it just the same and came to appreciate the generous nature of her gesture. It felt invasive when this person mentioned it. It was so tiny, so much mine and not to be noticed. But he wanted something I had, and by the end of the night, he got it.

When the sun started to come through the window, I left my room, staring regretfully at his white sneakers parked outside my door. I purchased the Sunday paper and a coffee and sat on a bench at the beach. I ran the night over and over in my head. What had I done? What had I allowed to happen? I prayed harder than I'd ever prayed not to be pregnant. I promised God I'd do anything, absolutely anything, if I didn't end up pregnant after this reckless episode. I vowed I'd kiss the ground if I got my period.

Then some days later, there was blood. Hallelujah! When no one was looking, I kissed the ground. But it wasn't enough. It wasn't my cycle. I started to feel nauseated every morning. I was going to have a baby, and I decided I was going to do it alone.

Margaret

When I discovered I was with child, it was as though a dark veil had descended on my life. All had seemed incredibly vibrant and enticing before. Spending time with Giovanni upon my return to Rome, I was moved to take him as my lover. While in England, Adam Mickiewicz, Polish poet and liberator, had urged me to rethink my chaste way of life. He implored me to explore the possibility of experiencing love in the bodily sense, a move I finally made, discovering the rapture of love fully expressed.

Now with child, I worried that my physical liberation had ruined my life. I had often longed to be a mother. I loved children and they loved me, but not under these circumstances. I was seized by the memory of a young woman I tended to years ago as she faded away after attempting to end an unwanted pregnancy on her own. In my predicament now, I felt much more compassion and little condemnation for that young girl. At the time, I held her to me, yet kept my emotional distance, recommitting to a chaste life, not willing to risk my life for sensual pleasure. Now I better understood her desperate actions and knew I was fortunate to be away and in the company of a man who would not abandon me—that I knew about Giovanni.

When I wrote to my friends and family, I hinted at troubled times for me in Italy. Yet I was careful not to say much, not to give any idea of the nature and magnitude of the situation. And they would never surmise it to be what it was.

My fear and darkness cast a menacing shadow over my life as I had known it and as I had so recently discovered it here in Europe. I was also afraid this pregnancy would kill me.

Without Giovanni's tender and unwavering attention, even from a distance, I surely would have fallen into an abyss, of which I can only imagine the depths.

Maria

My second eight-week teaching placement with Readak was in Lancaster, California, in the Mojave Desert. I was not sorry to leave Carlsbad due to unforeseen circumstances and pictured Lancaster as a sleepy little desert town with tumbleweeds, a couple of saloons, and maybe a pharmacy—like a movie set.

Whatever it was going to be, it was going to be starkly different than Carlsbad, the lush, quaint but exceedingly busy seaside resort town I had been in.

The school I worked at in Carlsbad was the Army and Navy Academy located on the beach. I was forced to raise my voice to be heard over the waves, and that was the least of my problems in attempting to be heard by those fully uniformed boys who stared at me like another bore, another adult they couldn't speak up or back to because this school was their last chance.

When it was over, I packed my belongings, said goodbye to my housemates, and drove away from the communal house in Carlsbad. Carrie, the only other woman in the house, and I hugged tight. She had just been diagnosed with multiple sclerosis and was scared. I felt terrible for her, but other than that, I was ready to leave that surfer-dude house behind.

Little did I know that my next destination would be my least favorite place I would ever live. I had secured living arrangements ahead of my arrival with a woman named Maria, who went by Yolanda, making it less confusing.

After taking the exit for Lancaster, I entered a most generic-looking city—Anywhere, USA—with nondescript strip mall after strip mall and neighborhoods of cookie-cutter houses. The houses, all painted in the earth-tone spectrum, required something unique hanging on the doors to help tell them apart. The only thing greeting me in Lancaster that I imagined were the tumbleweeds.

I drove around, squinting to see which house displayed Yolanda's number and finally pulled into the driveway. This would not be the last time I struggled with finding the right house, all of them looking so much alike. The mark of distinction at Yolanda's was a boat sitting on the desert sand in her backyard. If I hadn't been so immediately depressed by this place, I would have appreciated the humor in such a display.

Yolanda was nice enough. Really, there was nothing unkind about her. She opened her home to me, having room since all her children were grown and out of the house. She was rarely there, working a lot and often away visiting friends and family. I had the house to myself most weekends, which was preferable. My only real complaint was the number of Plug-In air fresheners she was compelled to have slowly melting in her outlets. It was nauseating. When I knew she would be away, I ran around the house and yanked them out. Otherwise, I felt like I was drowning in a vat of perfume—a terrible way to go!

I began to find my way around, locating a couple of diners to frequent alone. Unlike Carlsbad, I didn't seek out any friends and was fine with that. I didn't want anything personal here. The students at the private school where I taught were respectful and diligent. Most people who lived in Lancaster traveled the Antelope Highway back and forth to Los Angeles on a daily or regular basis. This town was known as a bedroom community, a place to situate and grow your family.

I drove the Antelope into LA one day to see my sister and her boyfriend, who were visiting there. There was a desperateness in my wanting to see them, not only because I missed family being so far away but because it had become clear to me that I had not left Carlsbad alone. It had become clearer why the Plug-Ins nauseated me and my strong suspicions were confirmed at the local Planned Parenthood. I was pregnant. I hadn't told anyone, carrying on in a daze, not wanting to face my altered reality. Suddenly, my plans had become undoable. Staying on with Readak for a second year, traveling abroad, and relocating every eight weeks did not seem like something I could do with a baby.

It was a relief to hug Ceil and Joe when I arrived at their hotel, to fall into the kind of ease you feel with family. We explored the city and dined in Beverly Hills. The next day we visited Universal Studios, an opportunity to wander around and revert to play. We boarded the earthquake subway, terrifying in that it was scary and made us scream, but we knew the entire time that we were safe. Simulations, precious in that we know they're not the real thing; still they bring us momentarily closer to the edge.

Our time ran out. Ceil and I were in the bathroom getting ready to depart, her to the airport, me to Lancaster in time for class. I knew this was the last chance to spill my secret. I remember her looking from the mirror to me with the caring and empathy I'd grown to expect, that I had received from her my entire life. It was a relief to share my dilemma, to shift a bit of my burden to someone I knew loved me and would stand beside me always. Maybe it was selfish to spring it on her that way. Maybe it was necessary. We parted with the shared secret raw, so much left unspoken.

After class, I returned to Yolanda's just as the phone rang. It was Ceil. We talked at length, discussing options and what-ifs, her comforting me and me growing stronger. Talking about the situation made it real, an awakening from the numbness I had felt since learning the results of the test. The words formed on my lips before they took up permanent residence in my mind: I am going to be thirty, I have an advanced degree and feel positive that I can support myself at this point, so anything other than having this baby now doesn't feel right. I had and would always be pro-choice, but here in this moment, in my life, my decision was clear. We said our goodbyes and love yous and I cried and cried, feeling scared and small standing in Yolanda's kitchen knowing my life was a taking a turn I had not anticipated.

Sitting on Yolanda's couch, drowning in decorative throw pillows, I called to inform Peter of this newly minted life. He extended a sincere offer that I come back, that we give it a try, see if we could make a go of it. I declined, feeling strongly that the best place for me was with my family in New England, where he, a New Zealander, did not intend to live.

Margaret

I WONDERED ABOUT THE ADVANTAGES OF MARRIAGE. IT seemed to rarely bring fulfillment and peace to either party, at least in its conventional mode. Many of my female friends—good, dear friends—ended up trapped in marriages that delivered daily grief and general unhappiness. This was disturbing, making much of me thankful that I was not married. Being a single woman, despite the stigma and difficulty, seemed the better option.

I especially witnessed dissatisfaction when the woman was bright, industrious, had goals of her own, and desired a life that extended beyond the domestic sphere so clearly marked for her then. Even if the man initially seemed accepting, this often changed and struggle ensued. There were so many reasons marriages turned sour and few options to dissolve an unhappy union.

Giovanni being ten years younger wasn't an issue between us at the time. When I considered years down the road, in my heart and mind, I believed I would not begrudge him finding another if he was moved to do so. I no longer felt the need to capture and hold. I had lived a liberated life, and marriage didn't seem to be a mandate where love was concerned.

I admit I had grown to value my freedom and would not sacrifice my goal to leave the mark I believed I was destined to leave, to be the catalyst I believed I would be. I may have chosen to move on from the relationship one day myself, and I believed the love Giovanni and I had for one another was far more malleable than the dictates of marriage.

Yet, we married. We married because we knew the clout it carried, especially if we returned to my home country with its rigid rules that, if not followed, created almost unbearable consequences. We didn't need to marry and we may not have if we hadn't felt it would make a remarkable difference, especially for our son.

This posed a conundrum for me, for if I married, it appeared I had succumbed to an institution I didn't fully embrace as is; and if I didn't marry, I stood to face scandal bigger than any I had ever faced. I was strong but at what price, with a child's future at stake? Those eyes, when they looked innocently into mine, persuaded me that it was best.

Maria

Ready to move on from Lancaster, I was informed that my next stop would be Spokane, Washington. That sounded good. I would drive up the coast of California and Oregon to my destination. As I started to map this route and hunt for a place to stay in Spokane, I received another phone call from Readak. How do you feel about St. Thomas, Virgin Islands?

I put my car in storage and flew to St. Thomas, to a climate I preferred—tropical and breezy with palm trees and lush greenery. I would have a co-teacher this time. What a pleasant surprise that was! Karen and I worked well together. We set up the program at Antilles School on the island, a school mostly of transplants from the mainland—Florida, to be precise. It was primarily a sea of blond hair and blue eyes and involved parents who lived in sprawling houses in the hills overlooking the aquamarine waters. Karen and I rented a small apartment attached to one of these houses. The view is still etched in my mind.

I did all the driving since we had a rental car and I was the one over twenty-five. Driving on the "wrong side" of the road, the roads narrow and winding, was frightening but thrilling. As we rounded each bend, we were treated to a postcard-perfect view. Once we descended into town, traffic crawled, making it possible to walk faster than drive, as there was only one main road leading to where we all needed to be.

One day, Karen and I were asked if we wanted to supplement our pay by substitute teaching in some of the schools on the other side of the island—the schools most of the locals attended. We agreed. In contrast to the predictability and flatness of the private school, the students at the parochial schools we were assigned to bubbled with an openness and laughter that was truly infectious. They wore their uniforms with pride and their smiles began in their eyes. When I left the school buildings on those afternoons and walked from that side of town past the cruise ships and the duty-free shopping, I was conflicted. The stark difference was amplified in this place. So much of the coastline of the island was off-limits with resorts and private homes. I didn't get to see the homes of the students at the Saint Peter and Saint Paul schools. I imagined them more cramped but much livelier.

I often agreed to drive Karen into town so she could use the payphone to call her fiancé. They were struggling because she had confessed to an affair at her last placement. She insisted she had only given the other man a blow job, out of respect for their engagement. She was adamant she had restrained from intercourse, which she believed would have been a true violation of their engagement. Her fiancé wasn't buying it, even after hours of explanation and pleading on the phone. It was painful to watch, but I had my own worries that kept me from absorbing too much of Karen's distress.

One night I called my brother and he informed me that Becky, his wife and my travel companion, had left him. My heart sank as I stumbled to find words to even try to console him. I told him I'd see him soon since my teaching in St Thomas was almost finished. Carmine replied, "Sooner than you think" and explained that he was flying to Los Angeles to meet me, claim my car from storage, and drive cross-country. I insisted that he had more important things to deal with, and I would be fine by myself, but he didn't want me driving alone, especially being pregnant.

It was final. He would meet me in LA on the day I flew in, and we would drive together, our goal to be back in New Hampshire for Easter.

Margaret

When defeat was evident, we had to flee Rome. The safest place, until we devised solid plans, was Florence. After securing an apartment, we set up a home for the first time as a family unit.

The winter weather that year proved assaultive. It wasn't the mild weather we needed to nurse our wounds and restore hope, but we made it through and discovered days, hours, and moments of great comfort and domestic happiness.

Many days were spent with the three of us occupying the same room—the only room we could sufficiently warm with the fire in the fireplace and from cooking on the stove. Although cozy, there were many times when the desire for space to think and write, that which most sustained me, was in dire need, and I was more cross at those I loved than I wanted to be. Despite this, I was able to make some progress on my lengthy work about Italy's valiant attempt at liberation.

Fortunately, we had friends in Florence who provided much-needed care and support, bolstering our confidence as a family out in the open for all to see. Friends grew to know and care for Giovanni and Nino, and my hope and vision for our future brightened.

One of our greatest joys in Florence was our close connection with the Brownings, Elizabeth and Robert. My friendship with Elizabeth, a natural one of mutual love and admiration, was one of my greatest pleasures. She had delivered a baby not long before our arrival, and our sharing the joys and challenges of motherhood strengthened our bond and the bond between our families.

We were sorry to leave such a supportive community in Florence, but I truly believed our return to the United States was important, and I began to imagine New York as our home, with the number of Italians settling there a part of this consideration.

A letter I would never see arrived from Waldo just after we departed Italy. In it, he pleaded for me to stay, stay and finish my book on the revolution, wait for the dust to settle on the scandal. He explained that with time and another best-selling book to my credit, people would be more forgiving. That would make our lives easier. It would make everyone's life easier.

Had I received his letter before we sailed, I doubt it would have convinced me. I was never one to back down because of others' judgment, and that Waldo knew.

Maria

When I stepped off the plane after my third and final teaching stint, there he was, my caring and hurting brother Carmine. Our embrace said it all. Things were different, way different than they had been only months before.

We hopped a taxi to the car storage, uncovered my rig, and headed cross-country. I didn't ask a lot of questions. Knowing

Becky had left him for someone else was enough. He didn't ask me a ton of questions either. Knowing I was pregnant and going it alone was enough. We listened to a lot of music, laughed, cried, and drove and drove.

We basically took the same route Becky and I had taken on our way out, with a few detours affording some novel landscapes and little towns to stop in. Of course, we had to stop often since I needed to use the restroom more frequently those days.

One of our first stops was the Grand Canyon. It looked and felt different now than when Becky and I had been there in August when it felt warm and breathtaking. We had spent time hanging around the South Rim, laughing at the tassel-eared squirrels and marveling at the views. We gazed upon this natural wonder with complete awe. When Carmine and I were there in early April, there was snow cover masking the full range of colors. It was colder than we expected, and all the silly squirrels must have been hibernating. The view attempted to captivate, but we didn't linger. We had a long drive ahead, and being home in time for Easter felt important.

We motored along the long, flat roads, the horizon as far as we could see out the front windshield, fields and pastures stretching out of the periphery of our side windows. There wasn't much there. It seemed flatlined and so did we. Just a stretch of nothingness. Yet here and there, a rusty little establishment would burst onto the scene, and I'd point it out with diligence, hoping they had a restroom. There was usually some food, a picnic table, and no shortage of local color to keep it real.

At the end of one particular day of relentless driving, we pulled off and found a hotel. We grabbed a quick bite to eat, wanting to get to bed early so we could get up with the sun. No sooner had we put the lights out, it began—a lightning storm like neither of us had ever experienced. It was frightening and amazing, lighting up the room for what seemed moments on end. A couple of times Carmine and I looked over at each other from our beds and saw the other bathed in a bright blue light. I couldn't tell whether it was the end for us because it was unusually terrifying, or in some Big Bang sort of way, a beginning.

Margaret

A big part of me didn't want to leave Florence or to leave Italy at all. But with everything I had been through, my heart longed for home, and the family I knew still needed me, the family I realized I needed as well.

I had no idea what the future held for me. For us. It didn't shine as brightly in my mind as I wanted it to, but most of my life was like that. The future always beckoned, and I willingly and courageously moved forward. And although always enticing, it rarely presented itself as golden. I supposed that was the life of the mind, of the creative, of the one never willing to be entirely satisfied with what was already known and established.

I realized that stepping foot back home was one of the biggest unknowns I would face. Holding hands with my boy, with my husband at my side, would supplant the usual image of me as a rugged, single woman. I would hold my head high, but I would no longer be solo.

The Brownings hosted a joyous gathering for us the night before our departure, and the next day Robert brought us to the boat with all our trunks and belongings. He helped us load everything onto the ship—the barque *Elizabeth*. While assisting us, he noticed how low the boat sat in the water from being weighed down with blocks of marble and other goods. He tried to convince us not to go, that this boat so heavily laden seemed unsafe.

I appreciated his concern but it was a cargo ship, designed to carry such loads, and I was determined to stick to my plan.

Maria

As we pulled into the driveway the day before Easter, we expected preparations to be well underway. Easter was a bustling holiday in our household. There would be cheese pies and homemade raviolis being prepared in the kitchen, and dozens of eggs waiting to be colored in the dining room, intricately decorated the Ukrainian way, using bee's wax.

We stepped into a kitchen of steamy boiling water on the stove and the rolling of pasta dough on the table, and were embraced with the warmth and security we had been raised on. There was much hugging and kissing and little asking for details aside for how our trip was. Carmine humorously emphasized our need to stop frequently for my bathroom breaks, and I mentioned how all-business Carmine had been so we could make it home for all of this celebration, and how happy I was now that he had insisted on that.

When the Easter festivities were a wrap, Carmine drove back

to Massachusetts to his apartment and his job, alone, and I settled into one of our childhood bedrooms upstairs, alone. I was turning thirty, pregnant, and unemployed. Not what I had imagined for myself. The next day I registered for unemployment and Medicaid.

Margaret

How much harder society is on women. Edgar Allan Poe could play the mongrel yet maintain his status, people focusing on his accomplishments and letting his uncouth behaviors fade or gather intrigue. With women, missteps, even if untrue, were magnified and allowed to color and darken all the good she stood for, all the accomplishments she had attained. And a man's word was taken above any woman's.

My friend Nathaniel Hawthorne penned a toxic entry in his journal about me. He questioned the legitimacy of my lover and child. He took who I was and what I had accomplished and proclaimed that I deserved to lose it all. He accused me of being a fake and believed that, in some way, this downfall he willed for me in his head was justified. It seemed he was playing judge, as his great-great-grandfather had at the Salem witch trials—a memory that haunted him, even compelled him to change the spelling of his name.

Years later, with Nathaniel and I both gone, his son, Julian, decided to publish this seething journal entry. Many sided with Nathaniel's bitter assessment.

Although Nathaniel composed this passage about me for his own dark purposes, Julian Hawthorne used it as an attempt to revive and secure his father's position. He wanted to reap any riches he could from his father's literary fame and works. To this end, he betrayed his father by publishing parts of his private journal. It was hurtful enough to discover that Nathaniel, after years of support, would write this about me, but it was even worse that his son would publish such hate years later.

Although the attack appeared to be personal, it was much bigger than that. It was backlash against the progress women were making as well as a means to discredit me, a leader and stunning example of this progress, to bury me deeper and deeper so few would ever care or know I existed.

Julian, a conman and felon, exploited his father to help keep women in a powerless place, which is where he kept his wife, the mother of his nine children; and his mistress.

Many women relished this slander and controversy, embracing Nathaniel's sentiments that I received what I deserved for stepping out of bounds. Perhaps this mess made them feel good and smug for not taking a risk, for accepting their more subservient position in society. But at that time I was dead and could not come to my defense. Others fought for me, some very hard. Most importantly, many continued the fight for women's rights, for human rights. The fire would never stop burning. Never.

Maria

Knowing I had choices may be why I didn't sink as deep as I thought I would. I imagined what I would be doing had I not ended up pregnant. I had planned to travel abroad with Readak, teaching somewhere else in this big, wide world. Instead, I was on Hooper Street, working with my sister and her husband in their small business making hummus and tabbouleh. But the ground felt solid.

The despair I escaped this time made me wonder if I had escaped deep darkness for good. Although grappling with heavy thoughts and feelings, there seemed a steady light ahead.

I was the recipient of a new sort of attention. I had space. I had time. I had a life growing inside me that seemed both the closest and the furthest one could ever feel to another. This life would be my responsibility, that I knew. But it also seemed like a miracle, little to do with me, hardly mine at all.

Sitting in the kitchen with my parents and family friends, conversing and playing cribbage was my new Friday night, smack dab in the heart of the home I had grown up in. There was no other place for me then.

Margaret

There was much merriment on the ship the night before we were to arrive in New York. It had been such a long trip, fraught with tragedy and incessant worry. Knowing we would reach land the next day lifted everyone's spirits and talk was lively and full of what we hoped to encounter once ashore. I relished in knowing that for the first time, I would hold my son with utter confidence in our lives together. Born in secrecy while the battle raged in Rome, left in the mountains where he nearly died of starvation, surviving smallpox at sea—oh, the joy of holding him in my arms at home, on land, feeling secure for once that he was mine to keep. I could finally believe he was not going to disappear the way Julia Adelaide and little Edward had. The magnificence of motherhood had secured its place in my heart.

Giovanni was lighthearted as well. Even though the prospect of living in America frightened him, he, too, was relieved to know we had made it. We had made it intact, this budding family. No matter what would come our way, we would handle it together, and it was sure to be less traumatic than what we had endured so far. Giovanni had begun to work through the pain of losing and leaving his own family and had come a long way in his resolve to start anew, to do the best he could, to learn English, and the ways of this new culture.

Our determination to return to Italy one day made leaving easier for him. For now, for my sake, he was willing to give this his all, to face it with the same grace and courage he had the battle in Rome.

I couldn't help but think ahead to our first days back, the leisurely catching-up hours with my mother and sister, hours to share at the pace one needs to make solid connections with new family. Oh, how our family had grown! These reuniting days loomed precious. I could feel their healing and heartwarming effect.

As we moved closer, even the seemingly daunting task of figuring out how we would make a living seemed doable, not as arduous as I imagined it from Italy. As we closed in on New York, all seemed lighter and more hopeful than it had from the other side of the Atlantic.

Maria

Suddenly, the nondescript date, July 19, had become significant, branded on my brain and looming large on the calendar. The due date of my baby. The baby I didn't expect to have.

In my childish black-and-white polka-dot maternity top, I felt inflated and untethered, like a fugitive helium balloon. Here and there, haunted by regret and beleaguered by feelings of stupidity, I imagined that had I come by this situation acceptably, it would be more of a cause for celebration. I would be said to have that glow. Instead, I sensed mine an awkward, cool reception.

Some outwardly embraced the turn of events without judgment, and their excitement about the baby buoyed me in the scarier moments. Despite the occasional scorn and self-loathing, I clung to something defiantly luscious that I alone could relish.

While walking to my doctor's appointments, I turned over and over in my head my altered life, how I viewed myself and how I perceived others saw me. I replayed my mother's response to my confession: "Why did you do this to me?" and she lamented how this predicament hurt her. How that made me burn with anger that she didn't see how it hurt me even more.

Yet this stubborn shame and hurt aside, I felt that the life inside me was so purposeful; losing so much seemed to be offering me something more in return; something derailing and unexpected could make me feel more alive than ever. The walks to my appointments, step by step, pieced together an altered mosaic of myself.

These walks continued longer than expected as July 19 approached and passed, and that date seared in my mind and circled on my calendar sat there until I had to look back at it. Ten long ticking days later, arriving barefoot at the hospital in the wee hours of the morning, this monumental bump in my journey decided to reveal herself because decisions would no longer be completely my own.

The new date, forever one of joyous celebration, was July 29, but that original formulaic due date, July 19, held its place.

Margaret

JULY 19, THE LAST DAY OF MY LIFE. SO CLOSE TO STEPPING foot on land in my own country, to returning home after a life-changing four years in Europe. Instead, I drowned along with my husband and son. Some said it was for the best, that returning to America married to an Italian and with a son many believed was born before we were married would have been a hell larger than what I experienced drowning in a shipwreck. They believed I was spared.

Had I made it home, had someone rescued us from that sinking ship, would not the love of my mother and dear siblings have been enough to sustain me? Would I not have known who my true friends were, those who would not turn away or accuse me of committing unforgivable sin?

It isn't as though I had never faced scorn and ridicule. I was strong enough to handle what would have come my way. Few knew the details of my personal experiences abroad because I never fully shared them and took them with me forever, swirling to the bottom of the sea.

There are several accounts of my last hours and moments. Who knows the truth? Even my own account is shaky from hours of unrelenting chaos. I wish I could change everything about the way I went down, but I cannot. How I lived and my vision for our world will always be most relevant and will always be my most valuable, enduring contribution.

Maria

WHILE LYING IN THE HOT TUB, I KEPT DOZING OFF BETWEEN contractions. Labor turned out to be excruciatingly long. And Theresa didn't leave my side. She stayed awake, rubbed my forehead, and kept me from losing my mind. With her on one side and the nurse on the other, it came time to push and our little girl was born. How many times do I call my little girl, Annie, by my sister's name? How many times am I reminded that Annie and Theresa share something beyond an aunt-and-niece relationship? Theresa witnessed Annie's birth. A mother does not always see what a birth coach, midwife, partner, or obstetrician sees—that first glimpse of new life emerging.

I saw my mother at the ironing board, positioned between the dining and living rooms, situated to lighten the drudgery with some television. My mother was always there, and I mean always. There when we got home from school every single day. The one who set the daily rules in the house, such as change into your play clothes, no TV until you finish your homework, no shoes off under the table, no swearing. The laundry, the dishes, the dusting, the vacuuming, making six lunches and cooking dinner. The one who made sure we had clean underwear, and our hair was brushed. The one I saw cry only three times when I was a child—when she broke her Corelle coffee pot, when Elvis died, and when her father passed.

Sometimes it was hard for me to give. Sometimes I doled out harsh words and judgment, something I couldn't take. Someone once told me that I couldn't take criticism, and he was right. If I let it in, I was worried I would shatter.

Now I was a mother. I had to do better.

Margaret

Premonitions often haunted me. Some came in the form of dreams, others by way of potent feelings. Sometimes they brought an overwhelming foreboding of death, reminding me, just in case I'd forgotten, that death was very much a part of life.

A recurring dream was one of my mother's passing. When I awoke in the morning, my pillow would be wet from crying. In my dream, I imagined the procession at Mother's funeral, and I imagined seeing her in the coffin. It tore me apart, for although my father and I were very much aligned—sometimes at the exclusion of Mother, sometimes in opposition to Mother—I always felt an undeniable attachment to her that became stronger as I grew older. Our bond redoubled after Father's passing, and we relied on one another to manage the household and the other children.

If I had had the chance to see her again on my return from Europe, our relationship would have been solidified in the way a mother forgives a child, in the way a mother loves a child, in the way a mother loves her child's child. The natural love we had for one another would have had the chance to come to full fruition.

It wasn't entirely surprising to not make it home. I had been forewarned by premonition after premonition, not only before I embarked upon this voyage but for years. I had seen myself go down in the darkness. I knew not when it would happen or exactly how. I had always respected the ocean, and it was a betrayal I would never understand. To be trapped in the swirl of my greatest fear, to at last come face to face with fear was indeed a most humbling experience. Dying in the vastness of the ocean and becoming one with its power and rhythm unites one to it for a long, long time. The longest time.

I lost my child that day, and my mother lost her child and the grandchild she would lay to rest but never meet.

Maria

When I held that tiny baby in my arms, life deepened and widened. The attention that flowed to her dripped into my veins too—a slow, luscious drip. It nourished her and it nourished me in a way I had never been nourished, in a nesting-doll way, she the tiny one that fit into me, me nesting into the next, my mom, who fit into the next, my grandmother, and so on. Women birthed by women birthing women. It seemed there should be unbreakable strength in that.

The years that followed my baby's arrival were full. They were busy in the way a person who becomes a parent becomes busy. There's more to do every hour of every day, folding little clothes, changing diapers, praying that you're making the right decision every time the air is pierced with a demand, a cry, or little legs flailing in the air. And when they get a little older and look into your eyes and ask why, you choose your words more carefully. Yeah, your days are busy. Your mind is scrambling. Your heart is full.

During the first ten months of my little girl's life, we lived with my parents, snug and secure in the proximity of experts. Then we moved into our own place and fell into our own rhythm—me and the youngest roommate I'd ever had.

Margaret

In 1843, as I readied myself for a position as a columnist for the *Tribune*, I took a seven-week detour to Fishkill Landing, a small town in upstate New York, where I secluded myself for the first time. There I took the advice Horace Greeley had given me to expand on a lengthy article I had written for *The Dial,* entitled "The Great Lawsuit: Man vs. Men and Woman vs. Women." For once I had the space, time, and distraction-free opportunity to create, to have my mind engrossed in a project without daily and domestic interruption. Although I was often fortunate enough to have domestic help and treated and thought of them as family, they too required direction, questions asked and answered, concerns ameliorated, and reassurance provided. They, too, liked to share their hopes and the events of their lives, especially when they realized I had an open heart and ear and a spark with which they were welcome to recharge.

Here though, in this quiet boarding house on the Hudson River, with my friend Cary in a separate room engaged in her own project, no one bothered me, no one questioned me except myself, and no one needed anything from me, even a particular look of reassurance. And during this treasured time, I completed what would be known as my greatest work, one I felt was an extension of myself, the first feminist book produced and published by an American woman and one credited with starting the women's rights movement in our country.

I quote what my contemporary Edgar Allan Poe had to say about this book: "*Woman in the Nineteenth Century* is a book that few women in the country could have written and no woman in the country would have published, with the exception of Miss Fuller."

I know Giovanni would have been the one to secure me such space as I went forward in life, willingly fulfilling the duties that had kept me from creating so much more over the years, freeing me from the caretaking details that had fallen to me, that fall to most women regularly. Yes, he would have spared me these, knowing I had so much more work to do.

Maria

I DIDN'T NEED TO HAVE A CHILD TO INJECT MY LIFE WITH purpose, but if you're searching for purpose and just happen to have a child, suddenly, in your arms is a bundle demanding focus. Soon she's standing in front of you with eyes and features that look familiar.

Along with raising my little girl, I was dating a man who had layers like the reflective mica I used to peel in my grandparents' yard. As I peeled, I discovered an almost mirror image, but at the other end of the rigid gender spectrum. Steeped in the same culture, he was bumping around in the same distorted, fun-house mirror maze I was.

My capacity for love and understanding had grown with having a child and holding this vulnerability in my arms and close to my heart. I knew I loved him when it hit me that if he left, I would be terribly hurt and sad but would never wish him harm and would always want the best for him. This was new for me, and it had to be love.

Our paths had been different. I had taken the college route, whereas he, after dropping out of high school, had earned his GED. I worked more from the head, he more with his hands. Where I backed away and avoided, he stepped up and let it rip. When the moments weren't good, I hid and he glowered.

He connected with me where it mattered, in my weaker spots, in the places that demanded examination. I didn't always handle these collisions well and neither did he. Initially, ours was a tumultuous relationship, two people in a struggle for the same thing, but by the grace of something much bigger than us, we were getting there.

Margaret

I LOOKED FORWARD TO LOCATING A HOME FOR THE THREE of us and, perhaps, my mother, who had been spending her days with one grown child or another since we had been forced to sell the farm in Groton years ago. It would have been ideal to have my mother live with us, and I envisioned Ellen and her children spending time with us as well since Ellery was often away.

With multiple women and an attentive father in the house, Nino was sure to get everything he needed, allowing me to carve space and time to complete my book and move forward with other projects. I had created enough of a name for myself that I knew I would have opportunities. There was a charge in the air that was certain to continue, and I was at the helm.

I imagined my friends would love Nino as I had loved the Emersons' Waldo, the Greeleys' Pickie, and the Hawthornes' Una.

In my vision, there was land and plenty of space for my mother's flower garden—her handiwork that provided my most colorful childhood memories. Nino deserved a beautiful place in which to skip and play, and I vowed he would be educated as well as the best of them, but I would not make the same demands my father made of me. My expectations would be high, but my means more reasonable.

And as I made this vow for Nino, I was reminded that my father's demands did not crush me; though his were the highest expectations, they produced some of my greatest gifts. Would I have been the woman I became without his vision for me, without him recognizing my potential and hammering home day after day that I was to see it through?

Maria

WE HAD BEEN DATING FOR A WHILE, AND NOT LONG AFTER his proposal in Puerto Rico, we decided to live together in one of his houses. This wasn't the only declaration of our love and commitment. There was a baby coming too.

Before Puerto Rico, we attended a party where friends teased that it was time to take our relationship further. One quipped, "If you see a lighthouse, that means you have to propose!" We laughed and Marty did propose to me at Fort El Morro, which hosts the oldest lighthouse on the island. Right after he proposed, it started raining. We ran for cover, wondering about such an omen, when a stunning rainbow appeared.

Lighthouses became a symbol of our union.

Not long after we moved in together, Marty headed out for a long-planned sailing trip with friends from work, from New York to the western tip of Florida. We were at that point in our relationship when being apart felt painful. We were so in love and enamored with our new life together. The lure proved too much for Marty to settle into the sailing adventure, so he hopped a train in the Carolinas to return home.

I was elated when he called to say he'd abandoned ship and would be arriving home sooner than planned. The next night there was a light tap on the apartment door. It was the happiest I'd ever been to see him. The potentiality of all lay before us.

We moved from apartment to house to apartment to house, chasing the glow, along with schools for the children and jobs for our careers. How surprisingly elusive that light can be, repeatedly facing the challenges of creating security in the storm and avoiding the ultimate pitfalls that can sink it all.

When we married, my sister Cecilia and her husband, Joe, gifted us with a beautiful painting of a lighthouse, the Fire Island Lighthouse on Fire Island, New York. This was where Marty had spent so many of his weekends as a child and some of the happiest and freest days of his life.

We hung the painting above the fireplace in the house we finally settled into and where we lived for a decade.

Margaret

It hit so hard we were thrown from our bunks. Although we had been aboard this ship for two months, in those first few seconds, I could not figure out where I was. I called out to Nino, whom I discovered was in Giovanni's arms. Giovanni pulled me in, and terrified, not wanting to face the cause of such a violent collision, we stood in an embrace.

With no choice, we climbed to the deck and discovered that we had slammed aground and were shipwrecked. The panic was abruptly hushed by the ship's crew. Their training to handle such an emergency set in, soothing those of us who were confused in chaos. In those early morning hours, dark and cold, whipped by wind, rain, and the occasional wave making its way over the deck, we were kept as calm as possible. This allowed me to summon my courage, making a pact in my head to hold out hope through this ordeal.

I was sure we were to be rescued. As the light began to rise, as it does rather early in July, it was apparent that land was in sight, yet the hurricane conditions did not let up. Shouldn't they let up? Don't storms pass? Isn't everything a lot easier to navigate in the light of day?

I consciously repressed my confusion and anger at ending up in this situation, knowing it would not help. But I wondered, how did the captain not see the light from the lighthouse and the other lights on shore? How had he missed the signals, the danger we were sailing into? These questions and their answers would make no difference to the situation we were in. It was a dire one.

I had been passing tests my entire life. There was no reason to think I would not pass this one—somehow, someway. Especially this one, where the stakes were the highest. I may not be able to do it alone, as I had often done in the past, but I had grown more accustomed to needing others. I had become more willing and open to accepting a helping hand—the helping hand I had been most of my life.

As the day wore on and our rescue seemed more doubtful, I didn't let on because I didn't want others to lose hope. I had to be their lifeline. I had to.

Maria

I LANDED A POSITION AT THE COLLEGE IN MY HOMETOWN, where I had returned to raise my daughter. This position and this child provided structure, allowing me to traverse the mornings, afternoons, and evenings of my new hold on life. The raising of this child was an unplanned but perfectly timed adventure, delivering mutual wonder and growth each day.

My work as an educational counselor for at-risk students—working with those who reminded me of myself, advising and guiding—provided mutual inspiration. It was as though I was dancing with myself, working to perfect the steps, showing them through who I was that it could be done and demonstrating to myself that it could be done without prolonged struggle. There was a better way. Not that one could escape all the lows, but one need not linger there so long.

I loved the man with the houses, the two of us navigating new relationship territory, neither having gone as deep as we would challenge the other to go. Soon another light entered our lives, a son. Life consisted of caring and cooking, playing and working. It was solidly good alongside its challenges.

I had been summoned to care for others, yanked from myself to step up and be responsible. To this I took a steady approach, channeling my mother and her mother. No matter the mood, no matter the circumstance, I rose each day to the challenge and was there for those who counted on me, both at home and at work.

These were midlife years—years when I grew without realizing it. Earlier in my life, I'd just as soon pull the covers over my head and never come out; the pains were startling and dark. Growth in later years was subtle and swaddling. As I nurtured others, I was nurtured. As I offered structure, I restructured myself at a steady, natural pace.

Finally, a proper unfurling.

And it began to build—this creative fervor. Like a tidal wave in super slow-mo, I longed for an outlet. It felt as important as my life. It was my life.

SIX

Margaret

LOOKING OUT OVER THE ROOMFUL OF WOMEN ATTENDING my Conversations, I was met with eyes flashing fire and future. Always a major proponent of education for girls and women, I now had roomful after roomful of women who chose to come together to broaden their intellectual minds, to expand their thinking and their lives.

I didn't know what to expect when I set up the first class and invited as many women as I did. Would a couple of women show up perhaps out of curiosity or kindness? But no, the room filled with the most eager women I could have imagined.

Although I had plenty to say, this was not a lecture. Yes, I presented the topic and led off, but the women themselves would search their minds and hearts for their interpretations and questions and use their voices to express these. These sessions were popular for both my presentation and facilitation and for what the attendees discovered about themselves by exploring the topics I chose for each week.

Sometimes I would assign a topic for them to think and write about at home and bring what they had written with them the following week to share. This did much to bring out the quieter ones in the group. Much was learned and sorted out by thinking and writing in advance of speaking. These Conversations by a woman for women, housed in a woman's shop—Elizabeth Peabody's—were a phenomenon that lasted over four years. When toward the end, I allowed several insistent men to join, the tone shifted, so I called an end to them.

The earnings from this endeavor assisted me in managing the household, always feeling obliged and committed to this end. Oh, how much more I enjoyed this run of Conversations to the teaching I had done previously. I learned much from the teaching experiences, but the taxing nature of such a lifestyle was not for me, and it crowded my days such that it made me ill. No, these Conversations were electrifying, for me and the attendees. These sessions were as effortless and life-affirming as breathing.

Maria

WORKING IN ACADEMIC SUPPORT OFFERED ME THE CHANCE to assist others daily, some days a small offering but always a positive force. A couple of colleagues and I noticed there were some on campus with unique needs, so we started an Adult Learner Program, fashioned after the good bones of other such programs already up and running and proven successful.

Here I experienced the real exchange of goods, the growth inherent in the open sharing of inquiries, ideas, and amazing epiphanies. Sitting in a room with twenty eager adults, discussing what we had read, examining meaning and form, we stepped into the sacred space where it was safe to explore, to share, to listen, and reconfigure. Such fertile ground I had never known, this roomful of others hungry to learn, to discover their voices and to share what they had to say.

As one student approached the podium, essay in hand, I sat captivated by the distinct glow around her head and face, her short-cut blond hair tucked snugly behind her ears, small gold hoops sparkling on her exposed lobes, the crisp outline of her adorably turned-up nose, clear eyes gazing earnestly at her classmates and me. When she began to read, her confident words and steady voice flooded the room, leaving no space unfilled. When she finished, holding her head high, there was not a sound in the room. "Thank you," I said. And I meant it.

They inspired me, these adults—some parents, some married, some divorced, some working full-time, some veterans, some managers and small business owners, some working their way off the streets. The range was vast.

I studied their open faces, their courage and hard work, their readiness and desire, their support for each other, for me, and me for them.

My years of bumbling into this, bumbling into that—none of it mattered anymore. There was something in the deliberateness of these students that spoke to me. Be it the first day of kindergarten or the first day of college as an adult, stepping up with confidence and purpose delivered that glow, illuminated the way. Being on campus until ten o'clock at night with these groups was a privilege.

Margaret

Nino was a charmer. He became buddies with everyone on the boat. Just a little under two, he worked the crew and other passengers around his tiny little finger. Because I was away a lot, he was used to finding his way, making his presence known, commanding connection and attention. A mirror image of his father, those big blue eyes and that look when he cocked his head, waiting for a response; he knew it was coming and expected that it would be good.

Everyone wanted to hold him, to snuggle him, to tease and play with him. On the boat, he was showered with love. After our captain on the Elizabeth died of smallpox, Nino came down with it, and all on the boat were frenzied with fear, worried we would lose our little boy.

His father and I were once again gripped with terror. I'd had premonitions, dark feelings that this trip was doomed, and had feared Nino becoming sick could be the basis. This scenario, once in corners of my mind, now supplanted other images that kept creeping into my head when I was both awake and sleeping.

All Giovanni and I could do was wipe him down with cool water to mitigate the fever, caress his soft forehead, rock his weak little body in our arms hour after hour, and pray—pray for the life of our sweet boy.

One day, he opened his eyes and looked directly into mine. There I saw my future restored. There I saw pure love and hope. Soon he was toddling around the deck again, the focus of all around him. Soon he was laughing again, squinting his eyes in the sun, cocking his head with anticipation. The dark veil had lifted and for a while, the sun came out.

Maria

Months after I had rushed my daughter to the clinic, I ran into one of the nurses who had been on duty that morning—that morning when I knew something had to be done. She told me my little girl was sicker than I knew. That she could have died. And I pretended I knew that, but I didn't and it took my breath away.

Not quite a year old, Annie developed red spots on her body.

The first diagnosis was chickenpox. That sounded reasonable. The spots tripled and began to blend into one another, becoming blotches. I whisked her back to the clinic where it was determined she was having an allergic reaction to an antibiotic she had been on. "Throw that away. Don't give her any more and give it time," they told me. "She will be uncomfortable, she will be in pain, and she will cry, but it will leave her system," they assured me.

I couldn't put her down. I couldn't make her feel better, swaying and swaying, singing and humming. She whimpered incessantly, all through the long night. As I paced the brightly lit kitchen of our apartment, too afraid to dim the lights, I felt alone and helpless. Every time I loosened my grip, she wailed. She didn't look like my baby anymore, her face distorted, her body a puffy red. With the sun's first peek, I brought her back to the clinic, where they raced her to the hospital so quickly I could hardly keep up.

The situation was serious and treatment options for one so young were controversial. Two doctors argued loudly in the corridor not far from me. But a decision was made, and my baby was soon on her way to recovery, her swollen little body transforming back into itself, her eyes looking like her, her wracked little body sleeping for hours on end, her mother collapsing in a heap and thanking the heavens for rescuing her baby.

Responding to this nurse months later, I pretended that I knew how close we had come and changed the subject.

Margaret

People couldn't help but remark at how different we were—quite opposites. Where I was perhaps overeducated, he was not. Where I spoke many languages, he spoke one and struggled with English. Where I was cerebral and often in my head, he was in the moment and more a person to do things, to manage the pieces around us. Where I embodied what most considered masculine characteristics, he embodied the feminine. He fussed over me while I worried about the world.

He was ten years younger than me and a naturally attractive man with gracious blue eyes, a calm demeanor, and accommodating ways. My eyes were dark and usually serious, my focus sharp and unwavering. He would maneuver around my moods and demands with care and understanding. I had never met anyone like him.

I could hatch a plan, the plan to keep our secret, the plan to disappear and have our baby away from eyes and the war. I could plan my return and how to assist once there. With all these plans, he would do what it took to see them through. I saw immediately that what he could do for me was valuable in supporting what I needed to do.

Giovanni and I were well-matched in our bravery. His family, once one of prominence, was in total support and employment of the Pope. Giovanni broke from them and stood for Italy's liberation, for which he was willing to fight and die. Being of strong Catholic faith, if his family found out about me, the Protestant he was involved with, they would have disowned him and cut him out of the family, both in support and financial backing. He was willing to risk it all for me from the start. I held him back from that, not wanting him to pay such a huge price for his involvement with me.

Once Nino was born, we knew we were going to have to share the news of our involvement and marriage, but our hope was it wouldn't hurt so much wrapped in victory. Of course, victory was not ours, and instead, we were wrapped in disappointment and fear.

Giovanni didn't look back. His mother had passed some years before and he missed her dearly. Now he was closest with a sister and was saddened to leave her behind as we headed for the States, but perhaps it was a favor. She wouldn't have to manage maintaining a relationship with her little brother or have her allegiance frowned upon by the rest of his family who had cut him out.

Although many were stymied by our relationship, it made natural sense to us. If only we had been able to share more of life together. If only our possibility of fulfillment hadn't been snatched from us so soon. If only we had had more time to work out the wrinkles.

Maria

I FELT MY FORTUNE DEEP IN MY HEART. MY CHILDREN AND their lives kept me inching steadily forward with the unfolding of time. They provided substance to my days, enhanced the highlights, and dulled the edges. Their joy added to my joy and their accomplishments delivered pride and happiness. Their laughter made me smile. Their playfulness and abandon reminded me of my own, and their struggles hurt and bruised me all over again.

There were days when this lifestyle felt a bit burdensome, days when I felt tired and tarnished. There were times when I let my restlessness rise to the surface and lost my patience. Then bedtime couldn't come soon enough. Or times when I was spilling over with worry about one thing or another. But these days and moments were not nearly as frequent and memorable as the golden ones.

When our boy was born, he looked at us with all the wisdom of the world. We were taken by the seriousness with which he studied us. What he had to teach us was immediately apparent. All we needed to know was in that gaze, that steady study in eyes just opened.

Margaret

I KNEW MANY WOULD WONDER HOW I COULD LEAVE MY baby in Rieti and return to work in Rome. And I suppose it was more than merely returning to work; it was returning to war. But I was always one who did what needed to be done, and to me, this needed my attention. Plus, I had to earn a living, especially now with a child to support. Don't get me wrong; it was hard, very hard, to leave almost newborn Nino with those I did not know. I had checked the situation out as much as possible, but I did not know folks in that area well, unlike others back home I had known for years.

I would be far away, not able to make it back even weekly. But I had to trust. I had to trust that these people would care for Nino in a way that exceeded the minimum, and them knowing the money would be arriving regularly would help.

Pulling away from the town for the first time after I birthed my baby, leaving him helpless and without his mother, and knowing he would be inconsolable for the first few days broke my heart and made me as sad as I had ever been. I could only pray that without me there, they would love him as their own, they would provide him with what he needed beyond the breast milk. I was never sure they did.

In Rome I was swept back into the fight, collecting the information and incidences and writing my columns for the *Tribune*. I never imagined I'd be covering a war abroad, but in an odd way, it felt right because the fight was for all I believed in. A staunch believer in liberty, I was filled with the noble and just reason for such an uprising. Although I despised war when the motive was for individual gain, greed, and power, a fight to free the oppressed was the only time a fight could be justified for me.

Trying to support myself in Rome and send the money for Nino's care was a challenge. I was no stranger to financial acrobatics and had managed for years to somehow make it all work, but it was stressful and at times consumed my mind. Yet I was able to block it out to an extent, produce some of my best writing, and hang on to the quality of existence I needed and thrived in.

What happened next became the worst experience I'd ever had tied to money.

Maria

My daughter's experience growing up was bound to be radically different than mine. As a single mother, the decision to work or not work was already made. Early on I patched childcare together, some days with her grandmother, my mother, and some with her great-aunt and great-grandmother—my father's sister and mother. These were nurturing situations, times to be spoiled by those who found her presence as precious as anything life can provide.

This patchwork could only last so long, and when fully employed, I searched for a full-time arrangement and found it in a home setting with Thia. Thia's nurturing of the few children she cared for along with her own was of the pure kind, the kind that indicated she possessed an infinite supply. When I picked Annie up on the last day she was to be at Thia's, we embraced with Annie in my arms between us, and all the way home I let out loud sobs while watching Annie's inquisitive face in the rearview mirror. Thia became a teacher at a local Waldorf School. A better choice for such a woman, mother of the Earth, I could not imagine.

From this point, I enrolled Annie in the top-notch child care center on the campus where I worked, and on breaks and holidays, she landed in various situations, some more nurturing than others.

When I was young, we only occasionally had a babysitter come into the house and she was usually Aunt Caroline, the one who would laugh so hard when she read our favorite story, "Not This Bear," that she would cry. We were befuddled. Who did that, laughed so hard they cried?

Margaret

When we arrived to pick up Nino, we were shaken to the core by what we found. Nino was near starvation, a shadow of his precious self, a little boy almost wasted away. Nino's caretaker had spent all the money I had sent on her own child, and our tiny, defenseless baby had been neglected and was near death. The disbelief and anger we initially felt and expressed had to be pushed aside to completely focus on our baby. We worked for weeks to nurse him back to health, to see him emerge once again as the feisty little one we knew and loved.

We experienced a wide range of horrible emotions after entrusting other adults with the care of our child and discovering that they had betrayed our trust while a helpless, innocent child paid the price. There can be no other feeling in the world to match this horror. We swore that Nino would never endure such recklessness again.

Our fight for independence thwarted for now, our child almost lost at the hands of heartless people, we dug deep into our reserves of strength and headed to Florence, where it seemed we would be safe until we sailed for what we hoped would feel like home.

Maria

One of our relocations occurred just as Annie was beginning fifth grade, so she would start a new elementary school that year where she knew no one. I pulled into the drop-off, and before I could hug and kiss her, she grabbed her backpack, stepped out of the van in her black boots and belted black dress— curly hair down—shut the door, and didn't look back.

I watched her walk onto the school grounds teeming with parents, teachers, and students, most reuniting after a summer apart. She held her head high as she approached the colored balloons signifying her teacher and class. I watched until the car behind me tapped lightly on its horn, and I had to pull away, my daughter's courage filling and breaking my heart at the same time.

And I realized that courage doesn't shield us from everything. Courage can keep us moving forward, even when the day seems dark and scary, even when regret and sorrow bring tears hot and wet down our cheeks, even when yesterday seems lost and tomorrow seems out of reach. When the ground we stand on at this moment is the most inhospitable we've ever felt under our feet, terra firma is but a step away. We will take that step, I realized, as Annie took her place in the line of fifth graders that early autumn day.

Annie reminded me of my little sister Theresa, the one I believed to be the most courageous, who as a small child could fill the house with her distress. When my daughter was four, I wrote this piece I titled "White Fox":

> It wasn't very often, not often at all, that the small white fox was taken from its box on the top of my mother's bureau. When the white fox was extracted, we all gathered around my mother for a touch, for a feel, for a chance to see those beady black eyes and to snap the small, triangular jaw a couple of times. My mother's small, artificial white fox stole was passed around for moments before she expertly draped it around her pearled neck and made her way from her room with all of us tripping at her heels.
>
> Rare. Rare that she and my dad went out, rare that they could find a sitter for the six of us. But occasionally it happened, and then the fox came out, and when the softest, whitest fox circled my mother's neck, I knew—I knew—we were in for a savory evening. A rare night released from the routine. A change in our short evenings, a lengthening of time for us, a yes to dessert, a yes to soda and chips. Six of us, round faces all in a circle around the low coffee table, hands in the bowl. A holler from the kitchen for a round of goodbyes. A different woman, the one with the fox, a mysterious person. Not the one that's always there early in the morning. Not the one who comforts us in the frightening nighttime moments, but a woman with her black hair up, red lipstick on, the scent of perfume, and the heels, not the sneakers or slippers of home.
>
> Not very often did the fox come out, excitement for most except the tiny blond one, the one who

> cried for fear the mysterious woman would never come back. The one who looked in the closets, under the bureau, behind creaking doors, just knowing she wouldn't leave us, wouldn't leave us like this.
>
> Hands in the bowl, catching crumbs on wet fingers. The television shows usually forbidden to us, the bending of small rules, the shut-ups that went unnoticed. The evening sweeping into hours unfamiliar, sleepiness coming to us on its own. The tiny blond one always curled up on the couch, out before she's tucked snuggly into bed.
>
> As if miles away, I hear the comforting sounds of adult voices in the latest hours before dawn, knowing as I roll over to push deeper into the warmth of sleep, knowing the gentle white fox will be so carefully replaced in its box and shut securely in Mother's bureau. Secure in its place until, oh, the Christmas party, when it will rise again, greeted by us all. Our fingers running over it, our curious hands snapping its jaw. Our mother in transformation expertly arranging it on her neck, the tiny blond one clutching her leg.

As I drove away from the school that day, I caught one last glimpse of Annie in line and it hit me: They grow and stay brave. They're not born that way.

Margaret

I ACCEPTED THE UNIVERSE, AND WHEN I SAID THIS, NOT many understood what I meant. Predictably, I was ridiculed. The torch I held high continued to burn with the flame of truth and the courage of all those who dared stand tall, often alone, striving to lead and light the way.

Unbeknownst to me while alive, I helped pass this torch to Walt Whitman, who ripped the pages of my essay, "American Literature," from my book *Papers and Letters* and kept them for the rest of his life. My vision of what a true America and its writers, poets, and artists would be, at that time overly dependent and imitative of English traditions, caught hold of him. In this vision, Walt Whitman could see himself. In this, it seemed I spoke to him. In this, he caught the electricity I knew coursed through our veins and fired our hearts. Walt Whitman accepted the universe in the biggest way possible.

Some have quipped that well-behaved women rarely make history. But neither do the so-called misbehaved. The history of women has been quite dependent on women to assemble it and to save us from needing to repeatedly reconstruct what we had already worked so hard to build. To make it to the pinnacle, we would need to recognize and build on each other's work over time.

Like the ebb and flow of the ocean, it was not a steady path forward but we made strong and lasting progress together.

Maria

When I started to piece things together, when I began to realize the world was in disarray, that innocent people all over the globe were suffering from starvation, disease, the ravages of war, and insidious oppression, I was overwhelmed. When the colorful spread on famine in *National Geographic* didn't feel like it was on another planet, when the look in that hungry, sick child's eyes could have been that of my son, the feeling of helplessness and complete devastation for those suffering the most among us was crushing.

At a loss and wrapped tight in my daily existence, I decided my most potent approach was to be the best person I could be, every single day in every way possible. A much harder task than expected, I had to continually start fresh each morning, reminding myself of what should be an achievable mission but one that elusively slipped through my fingers again and again. Examining thoughts, actions, what I was and wasn't doing, and reconsidering what my entire life was built on was exhausting and often felt futile.

A staunch member of the daily grind, keeping up with the expectations and demands of a society such as ours seemed a feat in itself. I wished I had hundreds of dollars a month to donate to a worthy charitable cause. Such an approach to alleviating my guilt and sadness about the state of the world would have been easier than trying to be a good person.

With our daughter in college and son almost finished with high school, the structure of such an existence began to loosen its grip on me. I began to emerge with energy unclaimed, with a desire that burned beyond anything I'd previously experienced.

Margaret

It's true that the women who participated in my Conversations, held for years in Elizabeth Peabody's bookshop in Boston, were primarily middle- and upper-class women, some of the better-educated white women at that time. I had to start somewhere, and these were women who could and would pay to attend these meetings. I trusted that they would do good, however local, with their growth through these experiences. When I looked out at the faces of these women and saw their eagerness, their hunger, and their excitement at this opportunity to explore issues and ideas normally outside a women's sphere—to step out from their cloaked captivity—I truly believed this endeavor would serve the greater good, and in so many ways, it did.

These women were designed for the domestic sphere, but even there they were delegated as partially ornamental with the tradition of household help to cook and clean. Their job became to pose, to create the impenetrable façade of a happy home. Their lives were needlepoint and piano, teas and strolls through manicured gardens. Their lives were often hours and days of emptiness and longing, wonder and despair. Some recognized and understood that their lives were not their own. Their desire to learn and discover felt like a curse, so they kept it in, they kept it down.

Looking out at the women in the room, ready to spring from their seats, bursting with desire to explore the higher ideals and current events that we would thoughtfully and openly discuss, I felt like a true liberator. I was proud they were present, proud they had the courage and willfulness to be in the room ready to learn more about themselves, each other, and their world. I was thankful for the supportive men behind them—the men who didn't do everything they could to stop them from being present.

I appreciated these women, they appreciated me, and from this mutual foundation we grew exponentially. Conducting these Conversations solidified my belief in the utter need for quality and equal education for girls and women and that women needed to be the ones to see that this happened.

Although my father kick-started it for me, men were not necessarily going to, on their own, do this for us. Education was the big liberator, and oppressors knew that; we saw that script play out repeatedly. Whatever was denied us, we would find a way to access, especially when we worked together.

Maria

I'D HAD A LOT OF JOBS BUT MY FIRST BIG BREAK CAME WHEN I landed a job at the state college in my hometown after I had moved back to have my baby. That job put me right back into the building, formerly the hospital, I was born in. It put me right back on the land my Italian immigrant grandparents and their families and friends had lived on for over a century. The position at Keene State College helped move me forward while taking me back to my roots—the literal trees my grandfather had planted in the early 1900s.

I came to this position when my daughter was six months old and left twenty-five years later when my son graduated high school. I moved from it being a job—matching a student with a tutor and demonstrating note-taking strategies—to being a way of life—striving to help students recognize their potential and begin to grasp their place and purpose in this world. But when working with a student on a daily planner became exhausting, when back-to-back student appointments started to feel depressingly redundant, I knew it was time for me to leave.

When being in the building I was born in and on the land my father had grown up on didn't connect the dots, I needed distance to bring it home. It was not going to happen on the ground my grandfather tilled, on the paths my grandmother walked to and from church every morning, or on the grass my father played on as a child. It was going to take a break, a move beyond the obvious.

This extraction yielded big and small discoveries. Little ones, such as reminding me that my true favorite color, before mechanically repeating emerald green, is sky blue. And my true first memory was not in my kindergarten classroom learning how to properly hand scissors to my classmates but years earlier on the front porch of a house we lived in on Butler Court—the Beatles playing on the record player and my oldest sister strumming an air guitar over and over so vehemently that Mom scolded her for fraying the front of her shirt.

Margaret

As I matured, so did my writing. As I expanded, so did my writing. As I began to understand that the basis of this gift—this ability to see, know, write, and speak—was for a mission much larger than myself, I went with it. Writing for the *New York Tribune*, I had a large audience, a bigger one than I ever could have imagined in 1845. This was less about me, Margaret Fuller, and so much more about our country, the people, and the world.

In my position, I worked hard to present art, literature, and contemporary culture in an honest light, nudging our nation toward its own identity through these dispatches and essays. I examined our country and our progress through a lens of universal truth, highlighting the very good and illuminating concerns. I believed people came to trust me, to understand that what I relayed was not for personal gain; my motive was far bigger than that. My motive sincerely was to move us in a direction that benefited all, every citizen of this country—the enslaved, the oppressed, the indigent, the incarcerated, and every person arriving here to make a better life for themselves and their families.

Although exceedingly difficult as a woman, with the restrictions and demands that continually assailed me, to think big, to take steps to broaden my view, I knew how important it was. I knew I had to move out of my own way, to recognize the challenges and the limitations these barriers posed, and to keep pushing against them, rising above them. Knowing my mission was far greater than me was what provided the energy I required each day. Realizing that criticism came with the territory, I constantly put it in its place and did my best not to get hurt over and over again.

I committed to being one with the world, an active participant, and to be privy to what was happening in the nooks and crannies of this wildly developing nation. But I also worked to keep my head above the swirl of shock and despair enough so I could write and speak in a clear and reasonable manner. I sought to reach others in a human connection, to remove myself, my disgust and anger. I channeled those I had studied who had done great work and tried to place the stencil of what was right and fair over our current situations to demarcate where we had gone astray. This sometimes revealed that where we were headed was not the best direction.

When your ego pops, like a bubble, it bursts, and you are over yourself. You are now nowhere, everywhere, able to be your best and do your best.

Maria

My daily walking began as an attempt to shake the gloom. My need for walking arose from my confusion, the call to put one foot in front of the other to keep my momentum going. Self-conscious at first, over the years I became more and more oblivious to those around me when I walked. But I learned to keep safety in mind, always.

Walking from campus to the house I lived in about two miles down the road was doable. Even at dusk the road was heavily trafficked. It felt safe enough, and I had walked the route many times.

One night, from the corner of my eye, I saw a car pull over and let someone out. That someone started walking up behind me, so I moved to the left to let them pass. But he didn't. Instead he walked closer behind me and grabbed my crotch. I froze. Shocked, instinctively I swung around and hit him with my stiff right arm. He backed up a bit, and we stared hard at one another.

I turned and started to run as fast as I could, and when I looked back, I saw he was running after me, not closing in but running steadily in my direction. I turned and ran some more, noting the lights in the houses as I passed, imagining pounding on a door, disturbing dinnertime, but aware this was an option. Looking again, there he was, still coming my way. I was getting close to the road I lived on so I blasted it one more time, my breathing heavy and loud.

Before taking the left onto my road, I looked back one last time, and he looked smaller. It appeared he had given up the chase. Hoping he couldn't see me turn, I ran down Bartlett Road, entered the house, and slammed and locked the front door. Leaning there, I let my heart settle and never walked alone at dusk or in darkness again.

Margaret

When the fighting intensified, when the cannon fire was so close that I instinctively ducked while in my apartment, I couldn't go out. I knew my days of walking around Rome were on hold. I knew much of what I had loved about the city, the ancient structures and natural beauty, would never be the same no matter who won the fight, no matter who emerged victorious. But

I knew the devastation would hurt even more, so much more, if Italy did not gain its liberation.

For the first time in my life, I was not able to leave my home, step out the door, and roam about. Now the only time I left was to scurry to the post office to see if a letter had arrived from Nino's caregivers or go to the hospital to assist with its operation and to minister to the injured. I knew I was risking my life each time I took these treks, but both were worth the risk.

These walks were with my head covered and down, my focus on my feet moving as fast as I possibly could. The sky above and the trees around me would have to wait, for these situations did not allow for such luxuries.

With every gunfire exchange, every cannon fire, I cringed and feared for Giovanni's life. I didn't know at the end of each dark, chaotic, smoldering day whether I would see him again. I had learned long ago, over and over, that we never knew who we would lose and when. But in battle, the chances were so much greater that I would lose someone I cherished. It was terrifying, no matter the worthiness of the fight and the bravery of the individual.

Maria

It took me years to discover that walking without a Walkman or Discman pumping pop music into my ears was enjoyable and worthwhile; that when you walk to escape, you are escaping, not benefiting in the way I do now or others perhaps did before there was a way to blast music into ears on the go. When I walked with music, it was another form of distraction. Yes, it was good physical exercise; yes, it was uplifting and could shift my mood temporarily, but it wasn't feeding me in the way walking came to feed me as time went on.

My husband had gotten me a Discman but it soon fell out of fashion, and I looked like an idiot walking around with what looked like a saucer in my hand. I ditched that, and aside from a short stint with an iPod orchestrated by my daughter, I started to walk with nothing. No music. No distraction. I've been hooked ever since.

We made our home in a handful of different places, and at each I quickly discovered a sacred route, some more scenic than others, but no matter to me. Each route offered its love, and if it wasn't scenic, blame it on us, not the land, the precious land that would be as naturally beautiful as it could be if left alone.

Over time, I became more in tune with the subtle beauty of the ribbons of nature we left around our cities. I noticed the wildlife that had adapted to these precarious situations, the squirrels and chipmunks that scurried for survival and played with one another. I admonished them near the road and laughed out loud at their entertaining antics. I listened to and worked to spy the birds in the trees and allowed the most subtle breezes to move me.

I was enchanted, and there was rarely a day I missed my walk.

Margaret

There were varying accounts of the last hours and moments of my life. Some said I allowed myself to go down with the ship, that I didn't try to save myself. And as a result, I took my husband and son with me, not allowing them the chance to be rescued either.

Some believed I was sure we would be rescued, that a boat would come for us. Why wouldn't it? Yes, the waters and weather were rough, but isn't this what they did, these men who had arrived on the beach? Wasn't it their job to rescue us? So I waited and waited and clung to the words I had written to my mother: if the boat sank, we would go down together—me, Giovanni, and Nino.

But there was another account, an account told by the deceased captain's wife, Mrs. Hasty. She reported that when all became wildly confusing, when I could not see Giovanni and Nino anymore, when the ship was at last breaking up for good, one of the remaining crew convinced me that my husband and son had made it to shore and now it was my turn. Mrs. Hasty said I believed at that final moment that we might be saved, that perhaps Giovanni and Nino had made it. So when this man told me to grab hold of the board, that grasping the board would be my first step to shore, I did. I latched on with all my remaining hope—hope that after all of this, I would join my family on shore. Gasping for air, my long, wet hair wrapped around my neck, my nightgown clinging to my exhausted body, Mrs. Hasty said that I believed I might make it, my husband and son ahead of me and me on my way.

But the instant I trusted to give myself over to the plank, the one I would desperately cling to until greeted by shore, I was swept away.

Maria

In graduate school, I discovered Henry David Thoreau. He was a no-nonsense man, a man brave enough to reject the inane in society and speak up against artificial values seemingly constructed to keep us in check, to imprison us in conventions, etiquette, and clothing. It didn't bother me that the house he built on Walden Pond and moved into on July 4, where he lived for two years relatively alone, away from immediate society, was funded by his friend Waldo. He still did it, and he, more than others, lived life according to his own beliefs and values. Of course this was before I rediscovered Margaret, also driven by her own beliefs and values, before I realized it was even more of a challenge for her than him.

Professor Lebeaux lined up a field trip, one of the only field trips I ever went on in college, to Walden Pond, to the site where Henry's little house stood and where a replica now stands. We peered through the Plexiglas windows, catching a glimpse of the economically arranged small space. Then we sat in the woods next to the pond, taking turns reading from *Walden* and discussing the man and his life's work. It felt both cheesy and sacred.

Henry David Thoreau was a master walker. He called it sauntering. Yes, it was sauntering that allowed you to observe, not be in a hurry, have no destination. I became a member of the Thoreau Society that day and received my tee-shirt—navy blue with gold lettering. The Thoreau Sauntering Society, it said. I had been a walker most of my life. Now I had become a member of an elite group of walkers—the Saunterers.

Margaret

I held out hope as best I could. It was overwhelmingly chaotic, assaulted by waves and wind stronger and louder than one can imagine. I held Nino as tightly as possible without crushing the young boy and tried to reassure the nursemaid, Celeste, who was lamenting loudly the fact that she had agreed to come.

For hours we held tight, looking to shore for signs of rescue. When it appeared my worst fear was going to happen, that we were going to go down together, I was convinced to hand over my boy with my last earthly prayer that one of the crew could swim him to shore. The chances were not good, but he deserved a chance to survive, the little one already having survived starvation and smallpox. When they pried him from me, I sank, soaking wet and freezing, exhausted and defeated. I hugged my arms around myself and dropped my head in sorrow. Giovanni and Celeste were gone. Nino was gone. All around me was darkness and death.

It seemed unfair that I should go down this way, but I knew well how life was. There were things I could control and others I could not. Nature was one I could not, so I begged for mercy. But she was not able to spare me. This I could accept more easily than the chains we put upon ourselves and one another.

If my baby and my manuscript had made it to shore, I would have accepted my fate more readily. My son hardly had a chance at life, and I had infused my manuscript with the fire for liberty, with our fight in Rome being a deep cry for freedom everywhere. My child and my work brimmed with potential.

I walked the earth for just over forty years, most of my steps in the direction I wished and needed to go. Tears of deep loss and great hope lap the shores of our world every day.

Maria

When I was a young child, I'd lie in my bed on the stairway landing at night and try to imagine where we went after we died. After death, was there only nothing? I tried to imagine what nothing looked like. I tried to get my head around the vastness of nothing. I imagined myself hurtling into outer space where I would keep going, barreling past the stars and planets into forever and ever. I couldn't imagine nothingness, couldn't imagine eternity. I'd lie there in the darkness, petrified because isn't that where my parents would go after they died?

Losing my parents was a great fear because I needed them and I loved them. I couldn't live without them. The thought of putting them in the ground—how cold it would be, especially in the winter—and being told that their souls wouldn't be there, their souls would be in Heaven. Heaven seemed like a good place to be, but what did Heaven look like and what did you do there? Was Heaven a whole lot of nothing?

My mother had a sewing box. It was rectangular with blue

embroidery of some design embellishing its beige fabric exterior. Somehow that sewing box became my visual representation of the soul. Maybe the words sew and soul became tangled up in my head. That box held thread, needles, and thimbles, and floated effortlessly through the cosmos.

Death was one of those things I went from not understanding to understanding all too well. Something I couldn't fathom then became the thing I learned to dread most, my greatest fear around death not being my own (no matter how unpleasant and scary that might be) but that of others.

Margaret

When Henry David Thoreau arrived on Fire Island not long after the shipwreck, I wished I was standing there to greet him. Instead he found very little of me and my family. Story goes, he found a coat believed to be my husband's and pulled a button from it to keep.

I liked Henry. He always seemed older than his age, so much wisdom for a younger man. He was someone who could take my feedback. As a literary critic, I had high standards and delivered thoughtful and honest criticism. Many writers had difficulty with this and hurled criticism back at me, much of it very personal. I'm sure being a woman made my deliveries all that more insulting to some. But Henry respected me and took my input, knowing it was not personal and was well-intended. Being at the beginning of his literary career, I hoped he found it of value.

It was not unusual for Waldo to call on Henry to do a task he either didn't want to do or couldn't do. Did Waldo not want to travel the distance to look for what was left of me, or was it too much for him to bear to be at the site where a treasured friend had died such an awful death?

Waldo knew I was working tirelessly on a manuscript about the Roman Revolution, and I had let him know that I thought it was the best thing I had written so far. He would have loved to have recovered at least that and to have worked with it rather than write my memoir as he and two other friends were convinced to do shortly after my death.

Only Nino's body was recovered and ultimately brought back to Cambridge for burial in the Mount Auburn Cemetery beside a cenotaph erected for us, which reads:

In Memory of
Margaret Fuller Ossoli
Born in Cambridge, Mass., May 23, 1810
By Birth a Child of New England
By Adoption A Citizen of Rome
By Genius Belonging to the World
In Youth
An Insatiate Student Seeking the Highest Culture
In Riper Years
Teacher, Writer, Critic of Literature And Art
In Mature Age
Companion and Helper of Many
Ernest Reformer in America and Europe
And of her Husband
Giovanni Angelo Marquis Ossoli
He Gave up Rank, Station And Home
For the Roman Public
And For His Wife and Child
And of That Child
Angelo Eugene Philip Ossoli
Born in Rieti, Italy Sept 5, 1848
Whose Dust Reposes at the Foot
of This Stone
They Passed From This Life Together
By Shipwreck July 19, 1850
"United in Life the Merciful
Father Took Them Together and in
Death They Were Not Divided"

Maria

For years we had visited Florida at least once annually, a smaller city we liked on the Atlantic coast, one that combined history and beaches. It seemed the ideal time to move. Our children were out in the world pursuing their own lives, and we wouldn't be that far away, a three-hour direct flight.

As we worked to shift our lives, I encountered a recurring vision. It was of me in motion, stepping forward in what appeared to be a grassy backyard. Draped in golden sunlight, the look on my face was that of tranquility. Such an image so frequently flashing in my mind must mean something, I thought.

Once settled and living there, I fell into a steady practice of mornings spent in thought, mornings engrossed in reading and writing, making connections and discoveries. On these mornings, I'd light a candle, the flame swaying in the early morning breezes coming through the screen wall of our small Florida room, my cloister.

There was a time, around graduate school, when my sister Cecilia and I would talk about how we wished we were monks, locked away and forced to be silent, forced to read and write all day long, called for simple, healthy meals, and then sent back to our practice again. We longed to strip our days of all the busyness, all the clutter, all the things that got in the way of expanding our minds, giving us space and time to think, to write, and to commune with the greats, those who had worked lifetimes to figure things out and had given us clues upon which to build, clues we had not received, not known, and had not seen the value in previously.

Oh, if only we had been introduced to this at a younger age! If only we had been coached and convinced that all this richness others had mined was ours for the taking, that we could run off with bags and bags of this gold, this most precious intel, this mind-altering treasure.

Being allowed to live silently and catch up was most appealing, but we had to work paying jobs, we had to raise families, we had to go to the mechanic, and pick up milk on the way home. Life cluttered us with all the little things we had to do every day, stole the moments and hours, and littered the mind with dozens of worries. But the abbey, the quiet abbey where silence and study reigned . . .

Some mornings it is so early that it is still dark in my little screened room—the bird talk, the squirrels rustling the stiff leaves, the cat meowing forever on the other side of the door. That's what competes for my mind when I come up for air, before diving in again, down deep where her voice and the words written about her awe and inspire.

I grew to love Margaret, Sarah Margaret Fuller, S. Margaret Fuller, S. M. Fuller, *. She's a sky full of stars. She's a long, meditative day at the beach. She's a woman who deliberately set one foot in front of the other day after day to tromp a fairer path for women, to clear the way for the good of all as best she could.

Margaret

I WOULD HAVE BEEN BACK ON AMERICAN SOIL FOR OVER three months. Organizers wondered whether I would have accepted their invitation as honored guest and speaker at the first National Women's Rights Convention. These conventions were annual follow-ups to the historic Seneca Falls Women's Rights Convention, which had taken place two years before on July 19, 1848—exactly two years to the day I died.

A moment of silence was proclaimed for me at the beginning of this convention, which was held in Worchester, Massachusetts, in 1850, not far from where I had lived the greater part of my life. Many still grieved my passing. Three of my good friends had embarked on a plan to write my memoirs—Waldo, James Freeman Clarke, and William Henry Channing. The biography they wrote about me, although not an accurate depiction as it rendered me less potent and radical than I was, was a bestseller for two years until *Uncle Tom's Cabin* came along. I was more than willing to step aside for that!

These rallies and conventions were not the way I typically chose to share my vision, not where I preferred to put my time and energy to move us forward on this front and others. But I appreciated the efforts of others and believed there was no one way to sustain the momentum in pursuit of women's rights and the abolishment of slavery.

Whether I was there or not, the first National Women's Rights Convention, taking place on those colorful autumn days of October 23–24, 1850, accomplished its mission magnificently.

Maria

Flying home from Israel after my stint on the kibbutz, I stretched out across three whole seats as the plane was rather empty, which was ideal considering the length of the flight. I had a year left to finish my undergraduate education, and when I returned to campus, I was carrying a tiny torch.

My sister Laura, the most practical of my sisters, had sent me a care package while on the kibbutz, and when I discovered it was a box of used books, I was disappointed. I put them in some sort of order on my side of the hut and started to read. In the Negev Desert, after a day spent picking kiwis and pears, I devoured these, one delicious book at a time. *A Zoo in My Luggage* was the first I read, about a man and woman who, fascinated with the exotic animals they encountered in other countries, brought a sampling home to England with them. Wow, how bold and strange, I thought.

As we sat on the veranda night after night, stars sharp in the desert sky, I listened to the other volunteers, young people from all over the world, debate with gusto and laugh from the gut. Sven from Denmark and Paul from Northern Ireland philosophized with apparent pleasure deep into the night.

I continued making my way through the yellow-paged books my sister had mailed me and to pause and look up at something I could not see but was beginning to understand was there.

Margaret

The frantic feeling. The flailing. The light above the darkness that you cannot get to. I had to let it go—the desperate will to live, the deepest fear of death. Then it didn't seem so awful. I accepted defeat when it was all but inevitable, after which the loss of me was no longer my concern. It became someone else's grief and, oh, so much more.

Following the publicity of my death, the Fire Island Lighthouse was deemed inadequate, mine far from the first ship to have wrecked on those shores. It was replaced in 1857 by a lighthouse twice its height with a start-of-the-art lens designed to guide ships more safely to shore. This new construction seemed a more fitting tribute to me than others. This lighthouse still stands beautiful and bold, thanks to the many who, despite new navigation devices, still recognize its value.

There was also reform to the rescue crews following my tragedy. Clearly, more needed to be done to save those drowning up and down the eastern shores than watching and waiting to make off with what valuables washed ashore. The lack of an earnest attempt to save those of us aboard the ship gnawed at those in charge and demand for change ensued. This was especially so after those who were there admitted that if they had known I was on board, a woman of such notoriety, they would have tried harder.

After the wreck of the *Elizabeth*, dozens of people were found guilty of plundering the goods that washed ashore, even personal possessions. This set a new precedent; hereafter, taking what was not yours, no matter the situation, was punishable.

These significant improvements for the protection of others reflected the way I lived and my constant desire and demand for us to do better, to care more.

My death and all that followed would not overshadow my life, my works, my value—nor should anyone's. Although some wanted to erase me, how I died was but an event, my birth and my death bookends to the impact of my earthly existence.

What lies between and beyond sustains, is the foundation on which we build, and is where we come together to continue this collective journey.

Maria

It had been years since I'd felt this low. I was turning thirty-nine and it was hitting hard. I called my sister Cecilia, now a psychologist, and shared my feelings, wondering why turning such a nondescript age would be hitting me so hard.

"Maria, you are no longer a young woman," she stated matter-of-factly.

I remember how powerfully that struck me. I was no longer a young woman. This was the last year of my thirties. A woman in her forties is not old but is no longer young.

As my thirty-ninth year unfolded, I decided I wanted to do something I'd never done for my fortieth and happened to spot an advertisement for a cruise out of Boston to Nova Scotia right over my birthday, May 22. I signed us up, and my sister offered to come to our house to stay with the children.

We boarded on May 21, and the next day we were out to sea the entire day, not coming into a port until May 23. My fortieth birthday was spent on the wide-open ocean, standing on deck, looking out over the vastness, feeling in a strange way that I was cheating time. How could I be aging when my feet were not on the ground, when I was being transported so smoothly and rapidly over the Atlantic? I felt weightless. It felt magical. But I also knew that if Mother Nature wanted to throw something our way, if we encountered one of her storms, our glitzy ship, with its stabilizers and massiveness, would still be vulnerable, tossed like a toy boat in a bathtub.

Captive on this ship the whole day long, I wandered around and found myself weaving in and out of the shops. I spotted a gold-by-the-inch shop and decided I'd treat myself to a gold chain necklace. I selected the design and thickness and had the sales clerk help me with the length.

After the clasp was attached and the sparkling chain was securely fastened around my neck, she tallied it up. "That will be forty dollars even," she said.

Margaret

A DEAR FRIEND OF MINE, JULIA WARD HOWE, POET AND social activist, orchestrated the construction of the Margaret Fuller Memorial Pavilion fifty years later on the beach from where I was observed to drown. It was beautiful and expansive, with benches along its perimeter and a bronze plaque. Julia composed the inscription, which read:

> To commemorate Margaret Fuller, Marchioness Ossoli, author, editor, poet, orator, who, with her husband, Marquis Ossoli, and their child Angelo, perished by shipwreck off this shore, July 19, 1850, in the forty-first year of her age. Noble in thought and character, eloquent of tongue and of pen, she was an inspiration to many of her own time, and her uplifting influence abides with us.

This pavilion went up in 1901 and was swept away by the ocean in 1913. The bronze tablet was never retrieved.

This beach, Point O' Woods on Fire Island, was not where I would stay. Where I died was not my resting place. Nor was the monument in Cambridge in the Mount Auburn Cemetery. That lovely monument is most important for hosting the remains of my precious son.

The electrical nature of creative thought and visions, powerful currents for human rights, equality, and democracy, continue to flow. They don't stay put. They cannot be buried. They cannot be held back or suppressed.

I was not ungrateful for these memorials and to those involved in the planning, construction, and dedications. The people involved were more important than the memorials themselves. They continued to illuminate our greatest common task, our trek to discern and operate within evident and higher truths.

Maria

ON LONG SUMMER DAYS, WE'D OFTEN RIDE OUR BIKES TO the public pool. It wasn't that close to our house. It was a few miles west, requiring us to pedal along a busy route, probably the busiest stretch of road in the city. We'd head out, towels around our necks and quarters in our pockets, enough to get into the pool and to buy a popsicle. My mother would wave and remind us to stick together and be careful. It was a dangerous ride as cars were the most dangerous machines ever invented.

We made it safely most days, except the day one of my brothers hit the curb with his pedal. We all heard the rub and the sound of his crash. Luckily, we were almost home, and he wasn't badly hurt. We all walked our bikes along with him in solidarity of his mishap and survival. For all our caravan bike rides to Wheelock Pool, we did OK.

Once there, we'd play in the water for hours, doing underwater handstands and somersaults, playing Marco Polo, and going on the slippery slide. The shrill whistle of the lifeguard caused heads to snap around to see who had done what.

Now, so many years later, I see myself climbing the ladder to the high diving board, standing on the very end, eyes closed, slightly bouncing. Maybe I should plug my nose? I decide to jump; I do not dare dive. Someone with one foot on the ladder waits below, not allowed to begin the climb until I go.

I want to turn back but that would be awful. Others are watching, counting with me, one, two, three, go. Go. Come on, go! I peek and it looks higher than ever, scarier than ever. Why did I do this? Why did I climb the ladder? I bounce a bit more to appease the crowd, to rock myself, trying to find some comfort in this terrifying situation.

One, two, three . . . I finally jump and reach out for something, and she's there. We spin in the air, in slow motion toward the water. We splash through, and she pulls me with her, swimming with determination to the side of the pool, waves in the water lapping us. I swim into her. She is gone. I climb out of the pool and step dripping wet onto the hot cement, looking up at the sun peeking through the tall, pointy pines that look like tall torches burning in the sky. I am strangely happy, grateful. It's as though I'm blessing myself without the hand movements I have been taught.

I race to get in line again, breaking the rules and running on the wet cement, my feet slapping loudly. No one notices me. I have become one of them. One of the not afraid who walk the high board now like a plank. When I get to the end, I bounce the board a few times for fun, and still I do not dive, but I cut the water feet first, with a fearlessness that makes us proud.

What should I ever have been but for you? I am not much now, but what I am, I owe in a large degree to your influence. You roused my heart with high hopes, you raised my aims from paltry amusements to those which tasked the head and fed the soul. You inspired me with a great ambition to distinguish myself above my fellows, and made me see the worth and meaning of life. Whatever we owe to those who give us confidence in ourselves, who make us believe we are something distinct and can do something special, who arouse our individual consciousness by an intelligent sympathy with tendencies and feelings we ourselves only half understand—all this I owe to you. You gave me to myself.

—James Freeman Clarke
letter to Margaret Fuller
March 1, 1838

RECOMMENDED READINGS AND RESOURCES

Brown, Arthur W. *Margaret Fuller.* New York: Twayne Publishers, 1964.

Capper, Charles. *Margaret Fuller: An American Romantic Life,* Volumes 1 & 2. Oxford University Press, 2007.

Channing, W. H., James Freeman Clarke, Ralph Waldo Emerson, eds. *Memoirs of Margaret Fuller Ossoli.* Boston: Phillips, Sampson and Company, 1852.

Deiss, Joseph Jay. *The Roman Years of Margaret Fuller: A Biography.* New York: Thomas Y. Crowell Company, 1969.

Fuller, Arthur B., ed. *At Home and Abroad.* Port Washington, NY: Kennikat Press, 1856.

Fuller, Margaret. *Papers on Literature and Art.* New York: John Wiley, 1848.

Fuller, Margaret. *Summer on the Lakes, 1843.* Boston: Little & Brown, 1844.

Fuller, Margaret. *Woman in the Nineteenth Century.* New York: W.W. Norton & Company, 1971.

Hudspeth, Robert N. *The Letters of Margaret Fuller,* 6 Volumes. Ithaca, NY: Cornell University Press, 1983–95.

Mitchell, Thomas R. *Hawthorne's Fuller Mystery.* University of Massachusetts Press, 2011.

Marshall, Megan. *Margaret Fuller: A New American Life.* Boston: Mariner Books, 2014.

Matteson, John. *The Lives of Margaret Fuller: A Biography.* New York: W.W. Norton & Company, 2012.

Murray McGavran, Meg. *Margaret Fuller, Wandering Pilgrim.* Athens: University of Georgia Press, 2008.

Myerson, Joel. *Fuller in Her Own Time.* University of Iowa Press, 2008.

Popova, Maria. *Figuring.* New York: Pantheon Books, 2019.

Von Mehren, Joan. *Minerva and the Muse: A Life of Margaret Fuller.* Amherst: University of Massachusetts, 1994.

Wade, Mason. *Margaret Fuller: Whetstone of Genius.* Clifton, NJ: Augustus M. Kelley, Publishers, 1973.

ACKNOWLEDGMENTS

Thank you to Shanti Arts and Christine Cote for selecting my manuscript for publication. I appreciate this opportunity to share my work.

I have had the good fortune to befriend incredibly supportive women writers since moving to St. Augustine. Thank you, Anne Baldridge, Lisa Mahoney, Paula Morton, Liz Robbins, and Marisella Veiga.

My sister Theresa Dintino is a constant inspiration and guide, as is my brilliant and wise daughter Annie Dintino-Cucchi, who believes it can be done and you can do it.

So grateful for Keegan Monahan, my thoughtful and multi-talented son who painted the cover art for this book, and Jenna Cea-Curry for working her graphic design magic, again.

And I thank my husband, Marty Monahan, for putting up with me on a daily basis and his fierce belief in me!

ABOUT THE AUTHOR

Maria Dintino has worked in higher education for thirty years, the first twenty-three at Keene State College in Keene, New Hampshire, as an educational counselor and instructor of first-year writing, and the past six years in the library at Flagler College in St. Augustine, Florida.

Maria is co-founder and writer for the Nasty Women Writers project, where she and her sister Theresa highlight women whose voices have been sidelined and erased from the fabric of our collective experience. Nasty Women Writers resists this shut down on powerful women's voices and claims #nasty as a stance of power, not the put-down often intended. Visit their website: nastywomenwriters.com.

Currently, Maria lives in St. Augustine, Florida, yet makes trips north whenever possible to visit family, friends, and especially her grandson, Jaxson.

Shanti Arts

Nature ▪ Art ▪ Spirit

Please visit us online
to browse our entire book catalog,
including poetry collections and fiction,
books on travel, nature, healing, art,
photography, and more.

Also take a look at our highly regarded art
and literary journal, *Still Point Arts Quarterly*,
which may be downloaded for free.

www.shantiarts.com